SUCCESS *The Original* HAND BOOK

SUCCESS *The Original*
HAND BOOK

JOEY REIMAN

LONGSTREET PRESS
Atlanta, Georgia

Published by
LONGSTREET PRESS, INC.
A subsidiary of Cox Newspapers, Inc.
2140 Newmarket Parkway
Suite 118
Marietta, GA 30067

Printed in the United States of America
1st printing 1992
Library of Congress Catalog Card Number: 92-71789
ISBN 1-56352-044-3

The book was printed by R. R. Donnelley & Sons, Harrisonburg, Virginia.
The text was set in Garamond Book.

Jacket design by Ian Barry
Book design by Lee Holbrook
Jacket photo by Parish Kohanim
Photo retouching by Joe Arenella

Dedicated to Cynthia,
who gave me her hand in marriage

ACKNOWLEDGMENTS

During every journey in life you meet outstanding individuals who give you a hand. Chuck Perry, my publisher, had the foresight to see the worthiness of this project and to give me the thumbs up. Robyn Freedman Spizman and Dr. Marianne Daniels-Garber pointed me in the right direction and helped me turn raw ideas into words you hopefully will hold on to. My wife, Cynthia, told me there was nothing to be afraid of. If the book was a success, we'd share the glory. If it wasn't, I would still be her favorite author. To my assistants, Laura Dobson and Mary Ganz, I applaud you. You kept marching forth working nights and weekends. And for the "little things," the so-called details this book wouldn't be possible without, I thank Babbit & Reiman Creative Director Crafton Stagg for her direction, Ian Barry for his cover design, Parish Kohanim for his photography, Joe Arenella for his retouching, Amanda Brannon, Randy Gragg and Thomas Richie for their creativity, and Michael Greenlees for his strong support and unswerving belief in success. I also extend warm thanks to my dear friends Barbara and Joel Babbit, Denise and Mark Connolly, Janet and Michael Gaffney, Sara and Armand Harris, Meg and Denis Reggie, Patricia and Neal Turen, and my Brother, Michael; to Eva Wright for proofreading, to Robin Fisher and Bobby Fisher, Esq., for his legal expertise; to Dr. Arthur Cohen for his love and wisdom; the Good family for their good wishes; and to my wonderful mother, who after reading almost every book in the world is qualified to be a library. Finally, I'd like to acknowledge my dad, who from afar had a hand in all of this, I'm sure.

CONTENTS

INTRODUCTION

Back in 1986, I flew to Tampa to give a speech entitled "You Are an Ad" to 500 people. A young man picked me up at the Tampa Airport to escort me to the hotel where I would deliver this highly publicized talk. Our conversation in the car was casual and my confidence was riding high. I had given this speech so many times I knew it by heart. "Who will I be speaking to this afternoon?" I asked. "The same group you spoke to last year when you gave the 'You Are an Ad' speech," he replied. I was speechless. The river below looked like a better alternative than the embarrassment I would face by delivering the identical speech to the identical group. My mind raced. I had two hours until show-time. So I checked into the hotel and while looking out my veranda I asked, "How did I get into this? How did it happen?" Then the answers came. I had done nothing wrong. In fact, I had obviously done some very positive things in my life or I wouldn't be here giving a speech! What if I were to share my discoveries and experiences about how I became someone they would pay money to listen to? I wrote down five beliefs I found in my heart that morning. Today they are in an easy to remember form contained in the five "finger" tips that comprise this Hand Book. By the way, the speech was an enormous success.

PLEASE NOTE: The Hand Book was printed with wide margins for you. Use the space to write down your thoughts, feelings and discoveries. Don't be afraid to underline or highlight phrases or pages that have special meaning to you. After all, what you get out of this book is more valuable than what I put into it. In school we were taught not to write in books. Unlearn all that, because once you personalize a book it becomes priceless.

PREFACE
Success Is in Your Own Hands

There are thousands of handbooks available today, but only one in the world you can actually count on. That's your own hand. It's always there and as simple to use as 1, 2, 3, 4, 5. Your THUMB reminds you to be thumbs up, because if you think positively, you will ultimately achieve what you believe. Your INDEX FINGER is the pointer. It points at what you want. Gives you focus. Once you have a positive attitude, you'll surely want a target to focus on. The MIDDLE FINGER you give to fear. After all, fear deserves the finger, and once you tell fear to get lost, you'll find faith. Your FOURTH FINGER calls you to go forth. Take action. Move ahead. Take the risk. Do it! And your LITTLE FINGER is a reminder that God deals in details and so must you. Put all five fingers together and you've got your very own Hand Book for success.

Since you were a child, you have been reaching for things. Not just toys, but love, warmth and security. To a three-year-old, those things mean success. Funny how we really don't change. Today we all want and need the same things. We desire the love of our family and friends. Respect from our peers. Acceptance of our ideas. Security in our job. Trust in the future and piece of mind. Success comes in many shapes. How do you grab it today? The same way you did when you were a child — by reaching for it. This Hand Book will teach you how to use your hands to pick up more than ever.

True love, faith, better health and greater wealth are now all within your grasp.

THUMBS UP

Thumbs-up people are positive people.

The energy they create attracts

all the goodness the world has to offer.

Thumbs-up people wake up every

day feeling excited and

go to sleep every night feeling safe.

GIVING THE THUMBS-UP SIGN ISN'T ALWAYS EASY

I oughta know. My right hand was paralyzed in a near-fatal car accident in 1975. While studying film in Rome, Italy, I was a passenger in a sports car that broadsided a bus at 50 miles an hour. The doctors said that with lots of physical therapy I might be able to raise my thumb. Once I did that, my other fingers would be sure to follow. I never forgot that. To the doctors it was a medical prognosis, but to me it became the meaning of life — get your thumb up and everything else will follow. Choreographing hundreds of bones, muscles and nerves in my hand was difficult enough, but keeping a positive attitude was the real hurdle. I couldn't just assume this would happen. I had to take charge. I had to keep in my mind a positive image of my hand moving. When the negative thoughts started to creep in, I had to chase them away. I had to see my hand moving. I had to believe that image could beat paralysis. I had to say to myself, "I can move my thumb, I can do it." The day I lifted my thumb was the most uplifting day of my life. And from that moment on I held the power of positive thinking close to me and have never let it go. I had won. My thumb moved because I believed it would and I made it happen. And just like the doctors said, my fingers followed the victor.

No gesture is more positive than a thumb pointing straight up to the sky. Soldiers do it before going into battle. Astronauts do it before going up into space. Even Lee Iacocca did it in his television commercials. How many times have you given a thumbs up? To your spouse at the beginning of the day? To your child after a great Little League game? Everyone has given the thumbs-up sign once or twice. The trick, of course, is to do it every day. To wake up in the morning and feel positive energy surging through your veins. To think of your thumb as a lightning rod for the human spirit. And to hold it up to the world daily. My mother always told me, "Thoughts have wings. And when they take flight, your thoughts will always bring back to you what you send out." She was right. I believe bad thoughts cause nervousness, colds, stress and insomnia. I can assure you bad thoughts bring disappointment, depression and defeat. They also invite others to ask, "Are you tired? Are you OK?" And you reply, "Fine," which is really an acronym for Frazzled, Insecure, Neurotic and Emotional. Good thoughts, on the other hand, take you a step closer to every goal you desire in life. They give you strength, health and something you can't purchase anywhere — happiness. Doctors agree unhappiness ages you and happiness revives you. Thoughts work for you or against you. It's that simple. Fear brings failure. Faith brings success.

Author Tony de Mello in his book *Song of the Bird* tells the wonderful tale of "The Golden Eagle." I'd like to share his story with you to illustrate the fact that what you see is what you are:

A man found an eagle's egg and put it in the nest of a backyard hen. The eaglet hatched with the brood of chicks and grew up with them.

All his life the eagle did what the backyard chickens did, thinking he was a backyard chicken. He scratched the earth for worms and insects. He clucked and cackled. And he would thrash his wings and fly a few feet into the air.

Years passed and the eagle grew very old. One day he saw a magnificent bird far above him in the cloudless sky. It glided in graceful majesty among the powerful wind currents, with scarcely a beat of its strong golden wings.

The old eagle looked up in awe. "Who's that?" he asked.

"That's the eagle, the king of the birds," said his neighbor. "He belongs to the sky. We belong to the earth — we're chickens."

So the eagle lived and died a chicken, for that's what he thought he was.

To think positively, you have to practice positive thinking. The way to do that is simple. When you think, you create. Your thoughts are seeds and your mind is the soil. So plant only what you want to blossom. You've heard the expression "sweet smell of success." Well, that's the blossom's fragrance. Centuries ago Buddha said, "Mind is everything. We become what we think." Jesus agreed: "All things are possible to him who believes." Ralph Waldo Emerson defined a man, I'm sure a woman, too, as "what he thinks about all day long." Shakespeare said, "There is neither good nor bad. There is only what we think." All of these people dedicated their lives to true fulfillment and the meaning of life. And they all agree — all of what we are is what we have thought.

Think of your thoughts as magnets. Whatever you think will be pulled toward you. Want to change the world? Change your attitude. At the 1992 Winter Olympics in Albertville, France, a news reporter asked world-class skier Alberto Tomba if he had ever won a gold medal with the number six jersey. Alberto held up his new skiing jersey and said, "Yes! Tomorrow!" The next day he won the gold medal.

UNLIMIT YOURSELF

What are you thinking right now? Are you saying, "That's fine for him — he's got it all. But what about me?" Are you thinking, "I can't. They won't let me. I'm trapped"? What about your job? Do you go to work each day casually saying, "This is my job for life. I'll never be able to_____. I'll probably die not having _____." Those are limiting statements. And when you look back on your life one day, you'll probably draw one big *blank*.

Right now it's time to fill in those blanks with your dreams. Go beyond your limit.

Many people still travel through life scared that a police car will pull them over and arrest them for going beyond the limit. In life you get a ticket for parking, not for moving. Step on the gas. Unlimit yourself.

Would you let a murderer into your house? Of course not. Then why let ideas that murder your goals into your head? I find it helpful sometimes to think of my head as a house. Every morning I straighten up the rooms, air them out and keep lots of flowers around to brighten up the place. How you arrange your house, or in this case the thoughts in your head, will "head off" the disasters you create for yourself. Be as selective about what goes into your mind as who goes into your home.

Point one. Never spend time with a thought you don't want to experience. Anything that isn't positive is abusive. Work with yourself until there is nothing in your house that doubts. Unfortunately, most of us aren't even aware of the negative thoughts we house in our heads — *I should have, I could have,* and *I would have.* If we were supposed to look back, we would have eyes in the back of our heads. And beware of the biggie: *I can't.* Over the next few days, write down every negative thought that pops into your head. Recognizing them is the first step toward getting rid of them.

Point two. Never talk about limitations. Even phrases such as "that's the top" and "the sky's the limit" are walls we create for ourselves. Don't worry. By the time we finish, the word "limit" won't even be in your vocabulary. You won't think about it, read about it or have any connection with it. And don't ever get in the elevator with it.

That's right, beware of negative elevator people who every morning wait until the elevator doors close to say, "Only eight hours left and we can go home." Or who at the end of the day say, "Just four days left until Friday." These elevator people don't elevate you. They de-elevate you. They are highly toxic and should be avoided. I suggest getting off on any floor rather than getting stuck in an elevator with one of them.

When you want to do something big, you must develop a mental picture. Then don't talk to anyone about it. That's because life is like a picture — if you overexpose it, it won't come out.

When my partner Joel Babbit and I opened our advertising agency, we had only one apartment, one telephone and one VISA card with a $9,000 limit. That was the only time we paid heed to the word "limit." We told each other that we were the best advertising agency in the world, and for the first few months we avoided talking to other people. We were afraid they might tell us otherwise. As long as we believed, we would achieve. John Lennon subscribed to this positive philosophy. When asked at a press conference how the Beatles became such an enormous success, he replied, "Because we believed we were the best f...ing group in the world." Joel and I also believed. As a result we, too, had one hit after another. This positive energy created the mental momentum that helped us become one of the strongest advertising agencies in the country. If we had asked other people how to get started, we would have heard theorems like, "This is the worst time to open a business." Or, "You need millions of dollars to pull this one off." And, "There's a formula for success I will share with you. For 10 percent." We could have sat around paralyzed by negative elevator thoughts, intimidated by the naysayers, the competition and the economy, and seen the days as blank pages filling up the wastepaper basket. We could have "analyzed the situation." BUT THAT IS LIMITING! Instead, Joel and I shut the door on the world and tapped into a universe of endless positive energy. We found it right in ourselves. Luke Skywalker called it "The Force."

Write your list of limiting thoughts in the down elevator. Then fill the up elevator with positive thoughts for each one.

THE FORCE IS AVAILABLE TO EVERYONE. ALL YOU HAVE TO DO IS BELIEVE IT'S YOURS. SOME PEOPLE CALL IT GOD. OTHERS CALL IT ENERGY. OTHERS CALL IT LUCK. IT'S NOT IMPORTANT WHAT YOU CALL IT. WHAT'S IMPORTANT IS THAT YOU CALL ON IT!

What do you think about before you go to sleep at night? Is tomorrow going to be a dream or a nightmare? It's important to dream before you close your eyes because what you fantasize about will often materialize in your dreams. So be positive. Your dream state is a powerful resource for you. One of my favorite exercises is to ask myself three questions, then go to sleep and get the answers in my dreams. Composer Francis Scott Key toiled for days over a piece that would commemorate the American Revolution. One night he heard a new melody in his dreams. The next morning he awoke to the "Star Spangled Banner."

In the midst of busy days, it's hard to dream. You're too busy getting through the day, but you must dream. Unfortunately, our school systems don't encourage daydreaming. Remember all the times your teachers called you back from a daydream? We were taught that we would fail if we did too much daydreaming. That's wrong. Dreams are good.

People always ask me, "How do you come up with those wild advertising ideas?" And I always say something very mystical, like I had a flash in the shower or God appeared. The fact is that my brain goes out to play. That's what creativity is — intelligence having fun.

And that's what I do for a living. I think positive thoughts about products and people and get paid enormous amounts of money. That's the pay-out for positive thinking. What's even more astonishing is the concept of advertising itself. Consider this: There are only four real products in the world — baking soda, jeans, perfume and tires. Everything else is made out of those four products. That's a fairly creative business. Five million products made out of those four. But to convince people that there's something different about these products takes lots of creativity. And that takes lots of positive energy.

Once when we pitched a dog food company, I wanted to do this TV commercial: An announcer invites the viewers to bring their dogs to the television set to see how good and delicious the dog food looks to them. Unbeknownst to America, I was going to blow a dog whistle onto the audio track. The Yuppies out there would never hear it, but the puppies would. Then the announcer says, "If your dog barks, buy it."

I never sold that TV spot. The lawyers killed it. But I did sell them "The Wag Guarantee — If your dog doesn't wag its tail when eating our dog food, you get twice your money back." I'm also trying to get them to consider kosher dog food for a Miami test market.

Convincing clients there's something different about your advertising agency takes positive energy, too. And this is critical because an advertising agency lives or dies on its new business record. Here is where the power of positive thinking really pays off. We never go into a new business presentation wondering whether we'll get the account. We go in knowing we already have the business. In our heads hangs a clear picture of us shaking hands with our newly won clients. The industry average in the United States is one win for every 10 pitches an agency makes. Ten percent is an unacceptable number to a positive thinker. Perhaps that's why Babbit & Reiman Advertising wins nine out of 10 pitches. An industry record, I might add. How do we do it?

Three years ago my advertising agency pitched a division of Coca-Cola. No new agency had been accepted into the Coca-Cola circle for more than 20 years. Between the time we were asked to pitch and the decision to give us the business, we had four weeks to prepare a presentation. We were competing against 10 other agencies. Inspired by creative guru Alvin Hampel, I had everyone in our office wear WIN buttons that month. Only WIN in this case was an acronym for Whip Insecurity Now. All the other agencies did lots of creative work, research and media plans. But only one person in one agency wrote the word "Coca-Cola" more than 500 times and circled the word another 500 times. Only one person drank Coca-Cola around the clock. Only one person sang the jingle around the clock. Only one person followed Coke trucks around the block.

Then it happened. One morning I looked in my rearview mirror, and there was a Coke truck following me!

By the day of the pitch, I truly believed we had the business already. My partner and I congratulated one another before even seeing the client. Then we went into the presentation room. Thirty minutes later we had caught the business because for 30 days prior we had caught the feeling. It worked. Instead of saying we'll believe it when we see it, we had said we'll see it when we believe it. We expected success and we got it. You've got to expect success to be successful.

This mindset works outside the business arena, too. When you go to a party feeling great, what happens? You have a marvelous time. That's because you are sending out positive signals. These vibes get other people's attention and make them desire you. Dance with you. Leave with you. Advertising works the same way.

THINK OF YOURSELF AS AN AD

The reason you buy a car, a shampoo, a shirt, a beer, an ice cream or a trip is because of the advertising. Print, radio, TV and outdoor boards have painted a picture in your mind that you want to associate with. Do you really think there's a difference in the products? Could you really tell one toilet tissue from another? Or is it Mr. Whipple who made you buy it?

People are no different. We are all created equal. But it's the image we create for ourselves that changes the way people look at us and act toward us. Like most advertisements, we, too, have headlines, visuals and copy. What's your headline? Is your visual appealing? Is your copy too long? Positive advertising sells positively. And nobody wants to buy a negative image. Here's how to sell the most important product in the world — you!

1. Your headline is what people usually see written all over your face. It's the first impression you make. So your headline must be positive. Does your headline say, "Pity me, I'm worthless," or does it say, "How to have a wonderful evening"? People love *how to* headlines. Whether it's how to fix a faucet or how to mend a broken heart, people want to know how. "Free" is also a powerful word consumers respond to. In a human being, free means a free spirit who will trust you and not judge you. This certainly appeals to me. Try writing a headline for yourself, and remember — if you don't get people's attention with the headline, you've lost them.

2. Make your visual exciting. If you have a favorite outfit, take it out of your closet and then give away the remaining clothes to your charity of choice. Then start a new wardrobe. There is no reason in the world why every outfit you own shouldn't be your favorite. If you can't afford a new ensemble, charge it. The interest you get from others will offset the interest on your credit card. Every morning,

wake up and get dressed as if you were going to meet the love of your life. Package yourself. In addition to designing your wardrobe, design your walk. Stand tall and proud. People always return damaged merchandise. Package yourself so your product stands out on the shelf from all the others. Don't forget the vital accessories — confidence, optimism, and enthusiasm. Without these you'll never make the best-dressed list. Forget them in business and chances are you'll be taken to the cleaners.

3. Terse verse sells. Nobody reads the copy in ads anymore, so what you say to people better be short, sweet, and to the point. Unless, of course, you're going to marry the person. Then long copy is essential.

Like any good ad, you must get someone's attention, interest, desire and action. Follow these advertising rules and there's a greater chance others will buy into you.

GROWING UP THUMBS-UP

As with most men, my mother was a formidable influence on my thumbs-up development. She lavished me with attention and infused me with confidence and an unswerving belief that I could do anything. As early as I can remember, she said, "Joey, you can do it. Joey, you're the best. Joey, you're a winner." She constantly played the song "The Impossible Dream" and was telling me to "just do it" long before Nike put the slogan on their T-shirts. I've read that when your parents are your biggest fans, you're bound to go on to bigger audiences. Picasso's mother said to him, "If you can become a soldier, you'll be a general. If you become a monk, you'll end up a pope." Instead he became a painter and wound up Picasso. Parents need to remember that being supportive means nurturing their children. Giving them confidence in themselves rather than conning them into doing something they want them to do.

For my ninth birthday I received a present that summed up my mother's belief in her son — a miniature White House. Just big enough for me and any visiting dignitaries from down the block. This White House taught me that if I wanted to be president, all I had to do was vote for myself.

During my high school days my thumbs-up attitude really got me places. I had a goal to be accepted to a very prestigious high school called St. Sergius. To an outsider, it appeared to be a school that was run by the Russian Orthodox Church. Four courses were taught in English and four courses in Russian. But to me it was where James Bond did his early training. My mission was to get accepted to this school without speaking a word of Russian. The faculty said I could join if I could learn the language within three months. Immediately I began reading Russian authors, bought every Russian record and saw the James Bond film "From Russia with

Love" 10 times.

When the interview rolled around, I knew how to escape from villains, bombs, traps and big, bad, busty women. I even knew how to cause a coup in a small country. But what I didn't know was Russian. Finally the dean asked me why I wanted to be a student at St. Sergius. I paused and said, "Sir, Chekhov said it best when he said (here came the extent of my Russian), 'A man is what he believes.'" The dean looked at me and shook my hand. I graduated from St. Sergius four years later, fluent in Russian. And though I never became a secret agent, I did learn a secret — people are what they believe.

When I applied to Harvard with an application full of honors, recommendations and four years of Russian, I wrote them that I wanted to major in international relations. At the interview I talked about potato blights in Russia and the Cold War. But in my heart I really wanted to be in the theatre. The interviewer noticed in my application that I had done a lot of writing, singing and dancing. Then he asked me if I was really sincere about a career in foreign relations. Something came over me. I got up and proceeded to sing "Consider Yourself" from the Broadway show *Oliver*. After the song, he told me he had someone else outside to see. I never went to Harvard. But that day I was smarter than anyone who ever did, because I believed in me. I knew what I wanted to do. Certainly it was impulsive! But I was vulnerable, open and confident. Thumbs-up thinking got me to the right place. In 1971 I was accepted to Brandeis University where I would write plays, sing and dance in musicals and help create a film department.

In 1977 my best friend in college, Neal Turen, and I wrote a musical called "Discovery—The True Story of Christopher Columbus." The underlying message of the show was: Don't wait for your ship to come in. Swim out to meet it. Take hold of your own destiny. And if you have a positive attitude, destiny will meet you half way. One of my favorite lyrics in the show was, "First you think it, then you've done it." When I was 24 years old, the musical was produced by people who believed in me. Again, because I believed in myself.

In 1978 I walked into the J. Walter Thompson advertising agency. I told them that I had watched the TV show "Bewitched" and that I could produce better ads than Darin Stevens. They just stared at me and finally said they would get back to me. I then went downstairs to one of their competitors and told them that J. Walter was considering me but that I preferred to work for them for half of what J. Walter offered me. I got the job for $100 a week. Enough for one Gucci loafer. (A pair meant you had made it.) Two weeks later I could say I had made it in advertising. Five years later I would become one of the youngest executive vice presidents of one of the largest advertising agencies in the world. Today I own 18 pairs of Gucci loafers.

In 1988 we sold our advertising agency for $5 million. People tell me it's easy to be a Zen philosopher with millions in the bank, but I've got to share something with you. You can't hug a checkbook. It's love that is the real power. My relationship with my wife is what has become paramount in my life and the source of my strength. I believe everyone will eventually discover, as I did, that what you find at the top of the mountain is what you brought there. And they don't take VISA on the top of the mountain.

HERO OR ZERO

Basically the world is divided into two kinds of people—thumbs-up people and thumbs-down people. Thumbs-up people always feel like Heroes. Thumbs-down people always feel like Zeros. Which way is your thumb pointing?

THUMBS-DOWN	THUMBS-UP
I have no love life.	I have a lifelong romance with myself. Who is worthy of sharing this bliss? Let's find out.
My family doesn't understand me.	I'm unique. I'm not a child anymore. I don't need permission to feel good.
My job is boring.	I've grown out of my job. I'm ready for more money, a greater position. A new challenge!

I don't feel well. I'm sick and tired.	I need to slow down. My body loves me and is telling me to take a break.
I've never done anything right.	My past is not my life. It's history.
I've got problems.	I've got opportunities.
I'm afraid. I'm getting out.	I'm excited. I'm moving ahead.

THUMBS-UP THOUGHTS

If your thumb is down, you need to work on getting it up ASAP. Complete this little list of thumbs-up thoughts about yourself:

I AM

1.

2.

3.

4.

5.

Now write three thumbs-up statements about your plans. Don't worry about how silly they sound. Write them down.

1.

2.

3.

THE THUMBS-UP WORKOUT

Of course, keeping thumbs-up thoughts takes practice. Here's a little program to make you a pro.

When you wake up tomorrow morning, make sure your thumb's up by making the following affirmations: "This is my day. The sun gives me positive energy. I feel good. Therefore, life is good." When it rains, I often stand out in my yard, naked, and let the rain wash away the fears I have picked up that week. Do make sure your yard is somewhat secluded.

Rx: Repeat your three thumbs-up statements three times.

Before Breakfast

Get your juices going by acknowledging how wonderful today will be. Look in the mirror and say, "I am confident, loving and open to the wonders of the universe. The people I come in contact with today are so lucky to be meeting with me. Their good fortune is spending time with me." Then jump in the shower and give yourself a mental shampoo. Wash all the negative thoughts out of your hair. Load your mind with positive affirmations. My favorite is, "I let go and let God." And don't forget to sing — outside the shower, too.

Rx: Repeat your three thumbs-up statements three times.

A Pause Refreshes

It's true. Lunch is not only the time to replenish your body, it's also a time to replenish your mind. During lunch take some time to get in touch with yourself. Go outside and have a picnic with nature. It may not be your thing, but for me there is nothing more energizing than climbing a tree. As children we loved climbing trees because they took us up. Why should it be any different now? If it's not your thing, take some time out to sit quietly and meditate. In this noisy world full of events, the act of meditation — even just one breath of meditation, where you straighten your back, clear your mind, breathe deeply all the way to your toes and exhale — can put you back in step with the world. Meditation is about being in the present. It allows you to focus on the greatest gift we have — our breath. One deep breath from your belly button to your shoulders fills your lungs with four times the oxygen they usually take in and gives you an enormous sense of well-being. Did you know the word "inspire" also means to inhale?

Meditation is like a glass of muddy water. If you let the glass stand, all the mud will sink to the bottom. What's left is purity. Ram Dass says of meditation, "The quieter you become the more you can hear." Prayer is speaking to God. Meditation is listening to God. If the term "meditation" bothers you, think of it as medication. Anyone does better and feels better when relaxed. Think about it. When do the little things really get to you? Not when you're relaxed.

After Dinner

Take a hot bath. But instead of thinking of it as just a bath, think of it as a tub of positive energy. Soak in it. Marinate in it. Enjoy it. After all, life shouldn't be a struggle. It ought to be a giggle. Close your eyes and visualize what you are and what you want to be. Avoid "I will" and "I'll try" phrases. The words "will" and "try" imply you haven't, and we can't have any of that. Keep the "I am's." Say I am wealthy. I am happy. I am in love. I am everything I have always wanted to be. Never "I will." Never "I'll try." Always "I am." Affirm that you have, not that you want. If you truly believe this, then it will come. Your faith must be so great that you no longer have to say phrases like "I hope," "one day," and that horrible word "if." Talk to your pillow again about confidence, joy, love and happiness. This exercise will also prevent hangovers.

Between Meals

Hug yourself. Buy yourself a gift. Write love letters to yourself and hide them around the house. Make positive affirmations. Dance to your favorite music in your underwear. Take a risk. Do smile exercises. Expect a miracle. Remember that your attitude determines your altitude. When someone asks how you are doing, tell them "terrific" and believe it yourself. And memorize the Ten Rules of Thumb.

Ten Rules of Thumb

1. Keep your thumbs up.

2. Picture the positive.

3. Focus on your strengths.

4. Eliminate your limits.

5. Meditate.

6. Party with positive people.

7. Ride elevators with the elevated.

8. Remember there is only one "U" in the universe.

9. Live YOUR dreams, not someone else's.

10. Throw "never" out of your vocabulary.

For those of you who wish you could live over again, I've got some bad news: This is not a rehearsal. In less than 100 years it will be all over. Your problems. Your job. Your mortgage payments. Your life. But remember, the only people without these worries are in cemeteries. And most of us die before we are fully born. You only live once, and if you go around twice, you don't remember anyway. So live every day of your life!

There is only one you in the universe, but your net worth is the same as everyone else's. All of us are worth 700,000 when we are born. That's the average number of hours we spend alive. How you invest them is up to you. The thoughts you deposit are the difference between a positive return and a negative one. You could say that when your thumb is up, your stock is up.

The Wright Brothers flew. Edison saw the light. Morse knew the code. And Ford had the drive. Positive thought is the single source of all success. As Virgil the philosopher said, "They can because they think they can." If you don't believe him, pick up Watty Piper's *The Little Engine That Could*. He taught us as children, "I think I can, I think I can, I think I can." This book ought to be required listening for first graders and adults. It teaches us early on about mind over matter. What else matters?

Perhaps the most wondrous thing about thumbs-up people is that they go to bed feeling safe and wake up feeling excited. Try it tonight. Think of your pillow as love, trust and joy. Then put your head on it. I guarantee you'll always wake up on the right side of the bed.

How do you feel? Thumbs up? Great. Now let's go for it.

A REAL POINTER FOR SUCCESS

Using your pointer finger allows you to harness all your positive energy and aim it at your personal goals. Your journey becomes shorter, keeping your eyes on the long-term goal. Free from distraction. Focused sharply on your target.

Some people use their index finger to scold. Other people find this finger in their noses. Successful people use this finger to point at what they want. Iacocca pointed at business. Madonna pointed at entertainment. Schwarzkopf pointed at Iraq. I pointed at advertising. You can point at love, health, money, anything. There must be something you want. Now just point at it. It's yours. After all, what's the point of having a thumbs-up attitude and not pointing at anything? Going through life with a great attitude but no direction is like a great archer without a target. You can't hit the bulls-eye that way.

DREAMING OR SCHEMING?

When I was in college, I was faced with a familiar dilemma: What would I do with my life? My grandfather wanted me to be a chief of neurosurgery. My grand-mother wanted me to be a Supreme Court justice. My father wanted me to go into business with him. My mother wanted me to be God. And my girlfriend's parents wanted me to be a dentist. I, on the other hand, wanted to be a filmmaker. I wanted to study with Fellini. I'll never forget my girlfriend's father asking, "He wants to work with a shoemaker in Italy?" It took courage, but in 1975 I boarded the SS *Leonardo Da Vinci* for Genoa. As my parents waved to their son, I gave them a thumbs up and journeyed to Cinecittà Studios in Rome, Italy, to tell Federico Fellini that I had written the greatest script ever. My own script of my own life. I didn't make any money. I didn't make any real career moves. But what I did make was priceless. I had made my own decision. And so must you.

WHAT DO YOU WANT TO DO? YOU'VE GOT YOUR THUMB UP. YOU'RE POSITIVE, OPTIMISTIC AND CONFIDENT. SOMEBODY ELSE WILL ALWAYS TELL YOU WHAT YOU WANT TO DO. BUT WHAT DO YOU WANT TO DO?

The elevator is going up. Where do you want to go?
WHAT DO YOU WANT TO DO?
Make your list right here:

SUCCESS or SUCKcess.

Sometimes I don't know how the word is spelled. So many people I meet, who are considered successful, are in a job or relationship they don't want to be in. That's why it's so important to define what success is for you. One thing is for sure: Webster lied. His dictionary defined "success" as "financial gain." Yet so many people who are financially successful are broke on the inside.

My favorite example of Webster's interpretation appeared on a recent cover of *Forbes* magazine. A 60-year-old man was pictured standing on top of a big rock. They must have borrowed Prudential's rock for the cover. What's more, clawing at the rock were his admirers — the losers — the VP's, SVP's, EVP's and all who wanted just to touch the ground the VIP walked on. Our hero was king of the financial mountain. He had worked day in and day out to reach his goal. And now his career was culminating with the cover of *Forbes*. The story talked about his planned early retirement at 60. Plenty of time left to enjoy his family and the fruits of his labor. After all, that was what he had worked for. But our Master of the Universe never tasted that fruit nor saw himself painted on the cover of *Forbes*. Instead, he appeared a week earlier in the obituary column of the *Wall Street Journal*. His epitaph read, "The heritage he leaves is a well-disciplined company." A warning to the person who sits on top of the world. It turns over every 24 hours.

My father worked every day of his life, except his last. On that day, as he lay riddled with cancer, he said, "Joe, don't work so much. It's not important." Come to think of it, have you ever known anyone who in their last hours said, "I wish I had spent more time in the office"? We can't live to work; we must work to live. A favorite toast of mine is, "Here's to living every day of your life." Think about it — living every moment. Still too many of us die without ever living. Don't tiptoe to your grave. Dance!

Peace of mind is knowing who you are and knowing that it's OK. This is real success. Popeye the Sailor Man is my idea of a true success. He sums it all up when he sings, "I am what I am, and that's all I am." Success, then, is knowing your real self. And knowing your true self is OK. Loving your true self is even better.

Don't let some 1980's concept of success suck you in. Sure, the money will come. But it will be at your or your family's expense. Instead, ask yourself, If I never got a salary again and could do anything I wanted to do, never having to worry about food, shelter or my family, what would I do? Once you accumulate this kind of knowledge, you'll have true wealth. And wealth stored inside you is safer than any CD on the market.

If you've done something just for the money, you need to work on your second finger and point to the goal that will bring you personal fulfillment. If you're with people you don't want to be with, point them to the door and point yourself in the other direction — to the people you enjoy or the job you enjoy. Even if it means a career change. Remember the peanut farmer and the actor who changed careers. Their names are Jimmy Carter and Ronald Reagan. Do what you want to do. Not what your parents said you should do. Not what magazine articles define as successful. And not what advertising says is "IN."

Being our real selves isn't easy because many of us already have been molded by the standards of the past. Many of us are actually living someone else's dreams. Our parents, like it or not, were patterns for us. They set the pattern and we followed it. Dr. Kevan Schlamowitz of Schlamowitz Presentations tells the story about a little girl watching her mother prepare a pot roast dinner. Her mother told her that the first thing she must do is cut the end of the roast off before putting it in the pan. When the little girl asked why, the mother said, "Well, that was the way my mother always did it. Let's call your grandmother and ask her why." The little girl's grandmother replied, "Well, that is how my mom always did it." The young girl then asked to go visit her great-grandmother to find out why. After some cookies and tea, the little girl approached the matriarch of the family and said, "Great-grandma, why do you cut the end off a pot roast before you cook it?" Looking across the three generations with a quizzical expression and a smile in her eyes, the great matriarch of the family simply replied, "Because I never had a big enough pot."

How many of you are making pot roasts your mom's way or working in jobs or living in a relationship that your parents think are perfect? If you are, you're living out their fantasies. Not yours. This is not the recipe for success.

One of the best lines on television was said by a character in "thirtysomething" who had come to the realization that she was living her parents' dreams. She said, "If you want to be happy, you've got to make believe your parents are dead." Don't misunderstand. She loved, adored and respected her parents. So much so that she was living her life to make them happy. Remember — live your life, not someone else's.

Being our real selves also means throwing magazines about artificial success to the wind. There are many fine articles out there, but the Cosmopolitans, Vogues, GQs, Esquires and Penthouses of the world create role models that send out the wrong signals. Add in advertising and you've got a three-ring circus. Billions are spent every year to tell you who you should be, what you should wear and how you should smell. It's not good enough to be you. You have to be perfect. This industry is brainwashing us. Ralph Lauren is a genius, but Ralph Cramden suits many of us just fine.

Remember the question: What would you do if you could do anything and be paid for it? And for God's sake, remember your answer. And remember this quote by e.e. cummings: "To be nobody but yourself in a world which is doing its best night and day to make you everybody else — means to fight the hardest battle which any human being can fight; and never stop fighting."

It's time you sit yourself down in the middle of your mind and announce the real definition of success. As defined by you. Here's your chance. In the circle, put the name of a person you feel is truly successful.

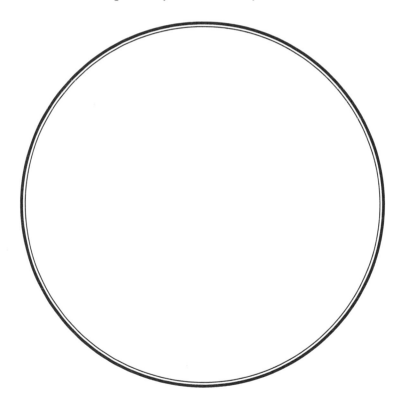

Who did you name? President Bush? Oprah? J. Paul Getty? Your father? Your mother? Your friend? I don't know who you named, but your answer tells you something about what you think is important. Is it money? Material goods? Power? What rises to the top for you? Again, I ask you, what is your definition of success? Don't think too much. Write what comes to your mind in the square below.

There are plenty of people who make just hundreds or thousands a month and still feel like a million. People who love themselves and love others.

THANK GOD IT'S MONDAY

At Babbit & Reiman we define success as, "The act of being excited about going to work." In fact, our employee manual has the letters T.G.I.M. on the cover. They stand for Thank God It's Monday. We are always thumbs-up — believing that in the end we will conquer the day because we believe so. During one new business pitch we were convinced our work was so "HOT" that we hired the Atlanta Fire Department to present the ads to the client. And we always pointed at what we wanted. Instead of a list of mom and pop video shops, we created a new business prospect list with RJR Nabisco, Cadillac, Coke and Trump at the very top. We won all four. When Rich's department store decided it would award the account to the agency that could do the best French promotion, my partner and I learned French. Only 10 words, but they were impressive ones. When we pitched Cadillac, we bought one to prove we believed in the car and in ourselves. That kind of investment could put an agency out of business if they didn't get the account, but we drove away with the win.

Perhaps my favorite story that demonstrates the power of the pointer was our infamous Del Taco pitch. Dozens of agencies were pitching for the account and it finally came down to just two. Us and *THEM*. "Them" was a monster agency, 20 times our size and real mean. They had it all except one thing — US! Del Taco, as most people know, is a Mexican restaurant chain. The pitch was in Dallas. Our office is in Atlanta. On the day of the pitch, both agencies brought creative work, a media plan, research documents and a slew of people from their respective agencies. But we wanted to make the point that we would do anything to get the business. We had painted a picture of success and couldn't take our eyes off it for a second. Idea! Three days before the pitch, I hired a mariachi band. After hours of rehearsing, they flew with me to Dallas. Our account people had found out that Del Taco's chairman, president and vice president would be dining at a Mexican restaurant in Dallas after they saw the two agencies' pitches. Well, their food came and with it came a mariachi band — not from Mexico but from Atlanta. As soon as possible, the band broke into "Ay yay, yay, yay, Hire Babbit & Reiman." The song was a hit. And the account was ours.

Recently I heard a wonderful story about one of this country's top radio disc jockeys. When he was 18 years old, he put an ad in the newspaper asking for any kind of job in broadcast journalism. Anything would do just fine. Anything. But instead of getting a job offer, he received more than 100 letters telling him what to do. He kept only one, which is now framed and mounted on the wall over his desk. The letter had only five typewritten letters in the middle of a white piece of bond paper.

FOCUS.

If someone were to ask me what has made our agency so successful, I would say we pointed at a goal and we loved getting there. Love is key, because nothing in your profession is more important than loving it. Except loving someone else.

This points us to another success we all want to have in our lives, and that is success in LOVE. Dr. Arthur Cohen, a dear friend of mine and a well-known psychologist, describes love as "where what you experience in life is like an apple dipped in honey," the freshness of life surrounded by all the sweetness life has to offer. One of the sweetest definitions of love can be found at the end of the long romance between Queen Victoria and Prince Albert. When the prince died, his wife whispered at the funeral, "Now there's no one left to call me Vicky." I define love as the only thing worth everything. By this I mean, I would give it all up for love. But before we call our love for others a success, we must first love ourselves. This is really what success in love is all about. Put another way, think about love as the ultimate self-approval. How do we do that? Just point at yourself and praise yourself. Approve of yourself. Trust yourself. Nourish yourself. Pamper yourself. Hug yourself. Buy yourself flowers. Give yourself what you want. Be in awe of yourself. Fall head over heels in love with yourself.

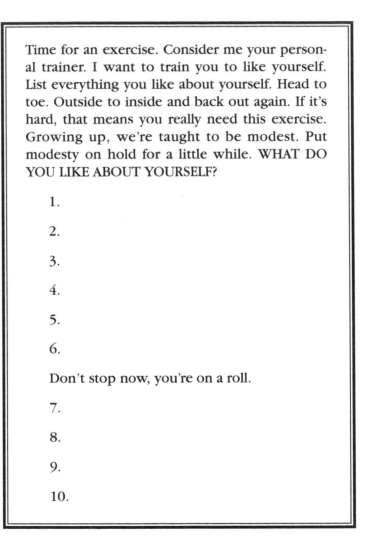

Time for an exercise. Consider me your personal trainer. I want to train you to like yourself. List everything you like about yourself. Head to toe. Outside to inside and back out again. If it's hard, that means you really need this exercise. Growing up, we're taught to be modest. Put modesty on hold for a little while. WHAT DO YOU LIKE ABOUT YOURSELF?

1.

2.

3.

4.

5.

6.

Don't stop now, you're on a roll.

7.

8.

9.

10.

Knowing your strengths is positive. Liking yourself is important. Loving yourself is even better.

Once you realize how wonderful you are, it's time to point again to a healthy relationship. That's one where the two of you do more than look into each other's eyes. It's a relationship where the two of you look in the same direction. To a place where trust is constant and the most precious things can't be seen. In Harold Kushner's book, *Who Needs God*, he recalls the legend of the sky maiden.

A West African tribe depended on the milk supplied by its cows. One day, tribe members noticed their cows weren't giving any milk. One tribesman stayed up all night to see what was wrong. Low and behold, a gorgeous woman descended from the sky on a moonbeam. She filled her buckets with milk and climbed back up the moonbeam to the stars. The tribesman was floored. The next night he would trap her. Down she came and down the net came trapping her with no way out. "Who are you? And what are you doing?" "I am the Sky Maiden and I am here in search of food for my starving planet. Please let me go. I will do anything you ask." The man, struck by her incredible beauty, said, "Marry me!" "I will," she said, "but first I must go back to my planet for three days, then I will return." "OK, it's a deal," said the tribesman. Three days later she returned carrying a box. She had one rule for the relationship: "I will be your wife and make you the happiest man in the world, but you must never look in this box." "Sure, no problem," he said. A couple of months later, while his new bride was in town, he was overcome by curiosity and opened the box. When she returned, he had an odd expression on his face. Immediately she knew. "You looked in the box, didn't you?" "OK, I did, but what's the big deal? It's empty." She then proceeded to pack up the few things she had and to climb back up the moonbeam. The tribesman pleaded with her, "Why must you go?" She looked back and said, "I'm not leaving you because you opened the box. I'm leaving because you said it was empty. It wasn't. It was full of sky and light and the smells of my home in the sky. How can I be your wife if what is so precious to me is emptiness to you?" She was gone forever.

Even when you're pointing in the same direction, love is work. And the more you put into it, the more you get out of it. I think of love as a kit. It comes with everything you need to build a beautiful relationship, but the right tools are a must. First a saw. The saw is used to cut away dead wood. You must clean up all your old relationships and resolve old hurts. These include your parents. Anything unresolved with them will come up in your own relationships. One way to tell if parents are lurking around is by the things our partners do that upset us. These are the things we have not forgiven our parents for doing. Especially embarrassing is when you and your partner find two sets of parents arguing in your bed in the middle of the night. Fears carried with you from childhood always emerge when it gets dark. Remember, you still may be your parents' sons and daughters, but you're not their children anymore. This will allow you to treat your partner like an adult, which always helps.

The hammer is used to nail down trust, faith and commitment. These nails need to be checked and rechecked. Every day I ask my wife, and she asks me, "How did I do today?" With some wood and concrete, you can build a fortress or what my wife and I call "the bubble." This is a place for just the two of us. No one else can enter. A safe haven where it's OK to be vulnerable and where intimacy abounds. A beautiful example of the bubble is an old movie entitled "The Enchanted Cottage." It's worth putting down this book right now and going to the video store to rent. Oh, be sure to watch it with your "bubble mate."

From the perspective of our bubble, my wife and I have learned some important things. The first is that when someone screams with anger, it is a cry for help. The second is to take responsibility for your own feelings. Never say, "Why did you do that? You hurt me," but rather, "I feel scared when you do that." Last, but most important, when in doubt, reach out. This is one of the greatest secrets we have uncovered. Try it. It never fails. Some of us, when in doubt, get out. These people ultimately lose out. I must say that marriage is the most refreshing part of my journey to date. Every day is filled with discovery, and many nights, as my parents once did, we dance under the moonlight.

Health itself is a success, so not a lot has to be said. But pointing at good health may prove to be medicine's greatest ally. Friendship and intimacy will help you live longer. Anger, suspicion, fear and boredom will help you die sooner. It's true, optimists are healthier. In fact, your attitude at 25 can determine your health at 65. Medical journals from all over the world confirm that positive imagery — "thoughts have wings" — boosts the immune system, shrinks tumors and is slowly erasing the phrase "terminally ill."

I once was told I would be paralyzed, but by pointing (I could only do it in my mind) to an image of a healthy hand, I am writing this book in long hand. My assistant was diagnosed with thyroid cancer — two nodules invading her throat and vocal nerves. Did I mention that she's a professional singer? Not once did she sway from a positive image of full recovery. In fact, right before her six-hour surgery, she booked a studio to record one of her latest songs. The doctors were cautious to pessimistic. She, however, was optimistic to inspirational. She came out of the surgery, called me and said, "Hi there!" Those two words were real music to my ears.

I have thought colds away with positive thinking (and a little chicken soup). I have made pain go away by meditating, and I have lowered my own blood pressure by fifteen points by picturing my blood switching from the fast lane into the right lane.

Pointing is also about choice. And the choice is

yours. Lots of people have it all and are miserable. Or have nothing and are happy. They push the happy or sad button. On the lecture circuit I heard a man talk about being a POW in Vietnam for six years. He lived in a six-by-eight-foot bamboo cell while I went to college, wrote a musical and got my first job. He said he was stripped of everything except choice. The enemy couldn't take that away from him. He chose to believe in a positive outcome. To hold on to the dream while others gave up. It was in that cell that he learned the power of choice and the enormous strength of his own will. Ambassador Bruce Laingen, who was also a hostage in Iran, says, "We're like tea bags. We don't know our own strength until we get into hot water." Both these prisoners pointed to freedom and got it.

No matter what you seek — health, wealth, love, faith or all the above — be sure to point to the stars. The worst that can happen is you'll hit a planet. If you keep your thumb up and point to your goal, you'll make it. The next time you're in a video store, pick up some old Michael Jackson videos. Find the scene where he raises his sequinned glove in the air. Notice anything? Maybe he's been making that point all along.

You've raised your thumb. Erased your limits. Defined success and identified your strengths. The only thing that can stop you is fear.

GIVE FEAR THE FINGER

When you give fear your middle finger, you're telling it to get lost. Only when you lose your fear will you find real happiness. Fear is an illusion and an illness. Reckon with it by leaning into it. This is the only way through it.

The middle finger is the tallest finger in your hand because it has the tallest order to fill. And that is to destroy fear. Giving someone the finger may be distasteful, rude and obnoxious, but giving fear the finger is wonderful, because there is nothing so bad or so dangerous in life as fear. When you give fear the finger, fear disappears. What's left is a clear road to your goals and your success. How many relationships have you abandoned in your life because of fear? How many career moves have you not made because they were too chancy? What about the fear of asking for more? Relationships have dissolved, wars have been fought and empires have fallen because someone gets scared. What about the fear of doing just what you and only you want to do?

If you have had these fears or have them now, you haven't been using your third finger. That's really all it takes. You see, fear is an illusion. It's not real. In fact, fear is the biggest lie ever told, and you and I are telling the lie to ourselves. When we feel fear, it is because we created it. We create negatives in our minds. Terrible jobs. Relationship disasters. And bad dinner parties. Fear is the darkroom where all these negatives develop. Want a positive picture? Stick your middle finger right out at fear, because the only way to beat fear is to meet fear. As Ralph Waldo Emerson aptly put it, "Do the thing you fear and the death of fear is certain."

When I was 12 years old I went to a sleep-away camp. One Saturday I saw all the "cool kids" in the camp signing up for an overnight horseback riding trip. I had never ridden a horse before, but I had been on a slew of merry-go-rounds and had never fallen off one of those horses, so I said, "Why not?" The counselor asked me if I could post and canter. I said, "Sure, but my gallop is a little rusty." "Perfect!" I thought to myself. "No galloping, the rest will be a cinch." We packed up and headed west — me, my horse, the posse and the unknown. I must have been on the horse less than five minutes when he was spooked by a snake. Off we went at a speed of 600 miles an hour. Something kept hitting my ankles. The loose stirrups. I held onto the horse's neck screaming at the top of my lungs. This must have deafened the horse because the word "whoa" meant nothing to him. My counselor caught up to me and saved my life and my horse's ear drums. "Never will I get back on a horse," I said. And I never did. At least not until the writing of this book. For our honeymoon, Cynthia and I went on a 200-mile safari through Kenya, Africa, on horseback. It was fabulous. I never fell off. I even galloped. Believe me, there's nothing like the freedom of riding through the wind except the freedom from fear. In two weeks I went from Out of Africa to Out of Fear.

There is no other way to live your life fully. Anything else is a compromise. Theodore Roosevelt said it a lot better than I ever could: "Far better it is to dare mighty things though checkered by failure than to live in the gray twilight that knows not victory nor defeat."

For years I've tried to write something like that. Recently I got my chance. An advertising magazine asked me to sum up my business philosophy into one sentence. Pretty major, huh? Everything I know and want to say into one sentence. Well, here it is:

"THE SAFE WAY IS A GROCERY STORE."

Tah Dah! It says it all — take the safe way and you'll end up with the title Head of Lettuce instead of Head of the Company. Even more dangerous are the people who have gotten somewhere and don't want to lose it. They minimize their future risks by pulling back their horns and their reins, forgetting the risks and boldness that made them what they are today. If you're not taking a risk at work, you're not doing your job as a human being. If you're not taking a risk in your relationship, you're missing out on what intimacy is all about. If you're not taking a risk, you're not taking home the rewards. Life is for the living, not for the "*If*ing".

Think of yourself as being on your personal road to discovery. If the road is well lit, you've got no problem. You can skip down the path, dance down it, run down it and even go down backwards. You're not scared because it's well lit. But there's a dark part of the road to discovery, too — the tunnels, the scary part. It is here that we must be the strongest because if we stop, so does our journey. That's what fear is — a tunnel. So it shouldn't surprise you that the best way out of it is through it. If you want to face your fears and fight your fears, this is the perfect place to meet them. Because it is in the darkness where we also meet the good guy — FAITH. The next time fear knocks on your door, send faith to answer it. You'll find no one there.

You've heard the expression "Keeping the faith." You've got to have faith in yourself. That means putting those negative thoughts aside and giving fear the finger. Your middle finger is a machete cutting off the limbs of fear at every turn. The road becomes so clear and faith so strong. Fear is a disease. The illness of the 90's. If thoughts have wings, these must be clipped, because negative thoughts that fly always carry back negative messages.

Here's an interesting tale that has happened to many people. I used to smoke cigarettes, and every time I got a sore throat I thought, "Oh my God, I've got throat cancer." OK, I was a little bit of a hypochondriac, but that's the fear I had. So I would say to God, "Look, if you make my throat better, I'll stop smoking." I would make all sorts of little deals on the side. My favorite was, "God, I hope it's a cold. I really pray it's a cold. Oh, please make it a cold and not cancer." You know what I was doing? I was making a pact with God to give me a cold. I got more colds than anyone else I knew. All because I made a cold the answer to my prayers. This is the power of negative thinking and proof that the only person who can hurt you is you.

Children, too, memorize negative messages without

their knowing. Author Stuart Wilde cites the nursery rhyme "Ring Around the Rosie." The original lyrics go like this:

> Ring — a ring of roses
>
> A pocket full of posies
>
> Atshoo, atshoo
>
> We all fall down.

Don't you find it peculiar that children have been encouraged to remember a poem, a medieval warning label, about the plague? Rings of roses under an armpit was a sign that you had contracted a fatal disease. Posies in your pocket was a preventative. The sneezing was a sign that you were checking out, and, of course, falling down meant death. This rhyme may have a purpose, but at best it teaches us as children that our energy drops every time we sneeze. What's worse is that the next song we usually learn is "London Bridge Is Falling Down." Unfortunately, as children we were taught to fear everything that was new. "Don't risk it." "Don't touch it." "Don't do it or you'll get hurt." Remember, these are fears for children, not adults. Yet many of us have not given these fears up. Do you know that when babies get scared they clench their fists? A clenched fist cannot receive. When adults clench their fists, they cannot receive either. Get the picture?

What do you fear? Take a moment to think about it, then write down your fears in the box below. Are you afraid of looking foolish? Are you scared to speak up? Are you afraid you will fail at something? These are common fears. So many people are out of work. Will this happen to you? Will you be abandoned by someone you love? Go ahead and write them down.

Now, what do you do if you have a fear of getting rid of fear? If you're so full of fear you're afraid of what life may be without it? Authors Peter McWilliams and John Roger believe you need to try everything three times — first to get over the fear, second to find out how to do it, and third to see if you like it or not. Here's another little trick I learned from them. The next time you tell yourself, "I'm scared," exchange the word "scared" with the word "excited." If you label it "excited" then your body says, "Gee, I'm excited." Psychologically they are both adrenaline rushes, but one leaves you with a *woe* and the other a *wow*. And for heaven sake, stop saying the word "should." It's a terrible word. No, it's the worst word. Worse than any four-letter word I know. "Should" is a word we were taught — "You should do this." "You should keep the job." "You shouldn't dress like that." Now here's the last *should* you should do: Go to your backyard, dig a hole about one foot deep, write the word "should" on a piece of paper and bury it while singing taps. Remember that "should" is a stick we beat ourselves with!

If your negative thoughts are chronic and you can't get to a therapist, the rubberband exercise may prove effective and inexpensive. Put a rubberband around your wrist. When a negative thought pops up, pull it.

Losing your fear takes concentration. After all, when was the last time you tried to lose something? Try losing your car keys. It's almost impossible when you try to lose them because you're thinking of losing them rather than of gaining something else. So if you want to switch jobs, don't say "I hate my job," but rather "I love that other job." Then you'll be spending your time finding what you love rather than losing what you hate.

Fear is all around us. News thrives on it, and for good reason. Three people dead makes a better headline than 240 million people alive. My wife, who is a news anchor for the CBS TV station in Atlanta, tells me that the rule in the newsroom often is: "If it bleeds, it leads." Sounds like bad news to me.

Then, of course, there's "Misery Loves Company." This ought to be a corporation made up of all the negative people in the world. It would be so big, I wouldn't be surprised to find it listed on the New York Stock Exchange. All you have to do to be hired is be scared. Be fearful. Be negative. And make someone else feel the same way. Today, there are local offices of the M.L.C. springing up all over the country. If you're part of one of these groups, quit. Without giving notice. Now.

Advertising is full of fear. Don't use the right breath mint and you'll get a divorce. You'll lose your shirt in business if you have ring-around-the-collar. Static cling will shock people. And God forbid your guests should see spots on your plates. I always wondered what "Fly the Friendly Skies of United" meant. Does this mean if you don't fly their route you'll fly over Beirut?

Fear is an addiction. Just like cigarettes, alcohol and drugs, many people can't let go of fear. Think about all the negative people and situations in your life. Would it hurt you to let them go? Can you let them go? Or are you like the smoker, the alcoholic or the drug addict who would hurt if an addiction were taken away? If it hurts to let go, you are addicted. People, in fact, can get used to anything, even if it's bad for them. Years ago a study was conducted with convicts who were incarcerated for more than 20 years. When released, the majority of them would commit petty crimes in hopes of returning to their comfort zone — the prison cell. We do this all the time, except for in place of cells we have fears. It's time to break out!

Fear of Losing It All

We all have a fear of failing at something at some point in our life. One semester when I was in college, my fears held a worldwide conference in my dormitory room. My girlfriend had left me for a dentist, so nobody loved me. I didn't know whether my screenplay would be recognized, so I didn't know if I was worthy of calling myself a writer. I wasn't pursuing my parents' career dream, so I thought I had failed as a son. And I was losing my hair. I called my mother to share my woes. I said, "Mom, my woman has left me. I don't have a job. And I'm losing my hair. Chances are I'm going to end up single, homeless and hairless." My mother said, "Would that be so bad?" I thought about it and realized it wouldn't be so bad. It was living that was important, and if I wasn't living then I was dying. And I was going to live.

When I changed my attitude, I changed my altitude. Everything was looking up. First, I stopped comparing myself to the dentist. He has to look down into people's mouths for the rest of his life. How much fun can that be? Second, I decided I was a writer. I didn't need permission from anyone. As Popeye would say, "I am what I am." Third, I realized that what was *in* my head was far more important than what was *on* my head.

The real irony about "losing it all" is that only when we let go of it all will we have nothing to lose and consequently not worry about losing it. So let go of everything, because you can't control anything. No one. No life. Not even your hair. You need to stay flexible. Besides, struggle is not positive. Every time we struggle against something we are reinforcing its reality. In effect, we are giving it control over us. When you hate someone, you are the person being hurt. As long as you stay angry at someone, that person will live rent-free in your head. Don't hate anyone or anything. Next to love, hate is the most empowering emotion. That's why unhealthy competition — the kind that makes you want to drop an atomic bomb on your enemy — always explodes in your face. When you love someone, the opposite is true. You are the person being helped. Do you want to let go of a grudge? Just think of the word. GRUDGE. The sound itself conjures up a slimy, grimy, dirty troll. Now imagine holding a grudge. Yuk. Let go of it. Your heart will be lighter and your hands will be cleaner. Sophocles agrees: "One word frees us from all the weight and pain of life: That word is love." For those of you who can't let go, remember this motto: The best revenge is moving forward.

Fear of Getting It All

For many, achieving success is the greatest fear of all. One reason for this is our education. Our parents and teachers tell us how difficult it is to make it to the top, so we don't. Other people fear change itself. And what changes our lives more than anything else in the world? Success. Still others are so afraid of not being highly successful that they dare not try, because if they did, they might fail. Then their worst fears would be validated.

I interview highly talented people every day who greet me, sit down in my office and spend 20 minutes telling me, without knowing it, why they couldn't be successful in the job I am supposed to offer them at the end of interview. Instead of talking about what they can offer the company, they want guarantees for themselves — like a contract for life, lots of money and a promise they won't work too hard or too fast. I think this all represents the fear of being fired, not eating and dying a derelict. People like this have a losing attitude and often go to interviews just so they can drop off all their bad baggage. Bags filled with fears. That's why I have a sign outside my office that says, "*Please leave your baggage outside.*" Fear cannot help you get hired. It can only prevent you from being fired from a job you will never get.

There are millions of fears in the world. They live in your head and your heart and they hate being kicked out. Here's a way to do it. Use the word FEAR as an acronym: *F*ind. *E*xplore. *A*ccept. *R*elease. "F" stands for find the "F"ear. We need to seek it out. Face it. Denying fear only makes it stronger. First we acknowledge the fear, then we must investigate it. "E" stands for "E"xplore it. Find out where it came from. Do you have a fear of dating? Do you have a fear of doctors? Do you have a fear of more money or more bills? Do you have a fear of not making it? Have you ever said to yourself, "If I'm not something, I'm nothing"? Exploring means finding out the origin of your fear. Finding out why you are afraid. The letter "A" stands for "A"ccept it. Lean into your fears. The best way out of fear is moving through it. So try doing what scares you. Then do it again. You'll find it less scary each time. You'll realize that what you fear today was caused by something many yesterdays ago when you were a child. Accepting your fear for what it was, not what it is, makes it disappear. That's where the "R" comes in. You are now ready to "R"elease the fear, forever. So release it!

A friend of mine went into a bank some time ago and was asked to sit down and wait a few minutes. He took a seat and watched the clock. Twenty minutes into eternity he got very depressed. His depression took him into the wee hours of the morning. His "F"ear was obviously associated with waiting. But once further "E"xplored, he realized his fear was from the past. As a child, he frequently waited for his alcoholic father to come out of one of the bars he had been in all day. Once he "A"ccepted this as the fear of a child and not of an adult, he could "R"elease the fear and consequently his depression.

Most fears you carry have traveled many years to be with you in the present. They don't have any use here. Send them back by remembering this:

FIND   — Identify the fear.
EXPLORE — Seek out its origin.
ACCEPT   — Do what makes you fearful. It can't
               hurt you anymore.
RELEASE — Kick it out.

Okay, it's time to give fear the finger. Using the FEAR acronym, list one of your fears in the box below.

```
┌─────────────────────────────────────────┐
│                  FIND                     │
│                                           │
│                                           │
│                                           │
│                                           │
│                                           │
└─────────────────────────────────────────┘
```

Now let's "E"xplore this fear. In the box below, write down your thoughts about the fear above. When did it start? How did it start? Who started it? Put the date, place and people associated with this fear in the box.

```
┌─────────────────────────────────────────┐
│                 EXPLORE                  │
│                                          │
│                                          │
│                                          │
│                                          │
│                                          │
│                                          │
│                                          │
│                                          │
│                                          │
└─────────────────────────────────────────┘
```

Next, let's "A"ccept the fear. That means deal with it. After all, the best way out is always through. Once you accept the fear you're almost home. Imagine doing the thing you fear. Now imagine being okay with it. Then imagine the fear disappearing. Poof! Doesn't that feel good? Now it's time to take action and do it for real. Make a commitment to bury fear by writing down a date and place to do what you fear most and conquer it.

```
┌─────────────────────────────────────┐
│                ACCEPT               │
│                                     │
│                                     │
│                                     │
│                                     │
│                                     │
│                                     │
│                                     │
└─────────────────────────────────────┘
```

You've succeeded. Now it's time to release fear. Sign your name in the box below and date it so you can remember that you gave fear the finger.

```
┌─────────────────────────────────────┐
│                RELEASE              │
│  I BEAT FEAR.                       │
│                                     │
│  Signature _____ Date ___ │
└─────────────────────────────────────┘
```

You have found a "F"ear, "E"xplored it, "A"ccepted it and "R"eleased it. Now go back to page 54 and pick another fear. Then repeat the exercise to exorcise the fear.

Dogs can smell it. Horses can sense it. And people can see it. Fear is as plain as the wrinkles in your brow. And you can always tell a victim — they look like they're about to be victimized. Young women are often told not to look scared or timid when traveling alone at night. The reason is simple — fear attracts trouble. Muggers don't like positive people, which might explain why so many muggers love New York. The bottom line is this: Don't act like a mouse or the cat will eat you.

The same is true in your career. People either carry themselves well or carry the weight of the world fearing that at any given moment they may drop it. You know who I'm talking about. And then of course there's the person who sits down at a conference room table and, regardless of the seat he or she sits in, that seat becomes the head of the table. Interview for a job with fear and you'll be fired before you say a word. Interview with faith and you'll find yourself making the decision rather than the interviewer. Basically it all comes down to people liking people who like themselves.

Countless books have been written about fear and health. Once again, fear can turn health into hell. Fear is the cancer of the soul. It raises blood pressure, causes high levels of stress, anxiety, neurosis and depression. It makes people smoke too much, drink too much, eat too much, work too much and can literally worry you to death. The irony of fear associated with illness is that we have the cure — faith. Or, put another way, the belief in a successful outcome. If you believe that the outcome will be good, then fear is absent.

Fear is very smart. It even has an agent that represents it. Two agents, in fact. They're called the Joneses. You know them. They live next door — the people you are always comparing yourself to. Let's see: "He makes more money. She's smarter. And skinnier! They have better jobs. They have a housekeeper. Their relationship is better. He has it all. She's got it easy. My window office isn't as big as hers. My car isn't as fast. I wish I had as much hair as him. They have a prettier house. Their children are in private schools. They go out more. She's younger. They have a pool."

Ninety-nine percent of all misery we feel everyday is due to one thing — comparing ourselves to others. Believe me, if you don't compare, your life becomes uncomparable. Stop asking the mirror who the fairest of them all is. You are. There is no one like you anywhere in the world. If you have doubts, watch the movie *It's a Wonderful Life*.

I'd like to admit something to you. I'm scared to ski. At least I used to be. While in Utah, a ski instructor taught me the secret of being a great skier. He said, "If you let me put your fear in my pocket, you'll be able to ski down this mountain or any other in the world." Now Cynthia and I book a ski vacation every year as part of our commitment to beat fear cold. And I can't wait to go.

Our marriage vows to each other were the greatest commitment of all. To trust each other. Our souls were fused by a positive, fearless expression of love. One which assumes a successful outcome. When you enter into such a contract with another human being, it's like putting out a contract on fear. Fear is killed. Faith is born. Now when fear rears its ugly shadow, we usually realize it's from the past. Then it cannot hurt us.

Here's an exercise that utilizes your middle finger with a little help from your thumb. As you know, success begins when you give yourself the thumbs-up sign. So this exercise should be a snap.

Look at your middle finger and visualize a fear that you have. Now say it in your mind and let the words travel from your head, down your neck, across your shoulder, down your arm, and up your middle finger until it's so small it can fit only in the tip of your finger. Now snap your finger. The snap you hear is the sound of your fear exploding. It happens every time your thumb goes up and your middle finger goes down. Repeat this exercise in the morning and night before you go to bed.

Your thumb is up. Positive thoughts are flying. You're pointing at what you desire and your fears have taken flight. Now you're ready to March Forth.

THE MARCH FORTH FINGER

Only when we march forth can we turn our ideas into realities. Action is the great separator between the Have's and the Have Not's. It turns ideas into I Did's. Action says, "Don't get even—get movin'."

March 4th is one of the holiest days of the year for me. Babbit & Reiman Advertising, in both New York and Atlanta, closes its doors on that day, for that is a holiday set aside to remember the most important thing in the world — marching forth! It is a day when everybody is encouraged to take action in their lives. To let go of the past. To break the hold of the super glue that binds us all to the fear of moving forward. Our fourth finger reminds us of that.

The best ideas are in graveyards. They are buried with the people who had those great ideas when they were healthy but never took action. Winning ideas that stay in our heads are losers. All of us have a book, a movie, a dream house, a prince charming, a great job within arm's reach, but we don't grab it. I, myself, start a new masterpiece everyday. Finishing them is another story altogether. How many masterpieces do you have waiting to be completed? Remember, getting started is the hard part. The rest is easy. If you don't know how to get started, find someone who does. "Learn how" will become "know how."

ACT AND YOU SHALL RECEIVE

Thinking is easy. Action is difficult. Thinking by itself will not create what you want. It is only a dream until action steps in and makes it happen. The meaning of power is not on Wall Street. The literal definition of power is *the ability to act*. Action is what separates the lovers from the loners, the happy from the hurting, and the winners from the whiners. People who take action take all. Who inspires you to march forth? Look around. How many doers do you see? Name them. Surround yourself with a band of doers. Then make sure you hear the music.

Perhaps "ask and you shall receive" ought be replaced with "*act* and you shall receive." History clearly demonstrates that people who have taken action have taken the world by storm. They dream by night and build by day.

Many years ago a cowboy by the name of Leonard Sly dreamed of going to Hollywood to become a big star. He was a positive thinker who knew what he wanted. I've heard he was fearless, too. But he just couldn't get his foot in the door of a big studio. Then one day Leonard was approached by a man who wanted to borrow his cowboy hat. The man said he needed it because he was going to try out for the part of a cowboy at Republic Studios. Leonard declined, packed his bags, drove to Hollywood, got the part, changed his name to Roy Rogers and rode off into the sunset with happy trails forever. My hat's off to Roy for turning an action into an astounding acting career.

In 1988, Babbit & Reiman was two years old and had made a creative reputation for itself but had not made much money. I decided this was the year to take action. On March 4th, I flew to New York in search of new business for the agency. After all, the largest accounts in the world have their headquarters in New York. This was the place to march forth. While there I thought I would drop in on my former agent. The last time she had gotten me a job, she had negotiated a contract for a modest $33,000 a year. But she was always a friend, so why not say hello? "Joey, how have you been? I know you've been doing some super work. Do you have any samples with you? There's someone here I'd like to show them to." I always carry a short videocassette with me in case I run into a new business prospect, so I said, "Sure." The someone turned out to be Matthew Allen, the chief financial officer of Gold Greenlees Trott, one of the world's largest and most respected advertising agencies. The five minutes I spent with him turned into five million dollars one month later when his company bought Babbit & Reiman.

MEET ABE

Then there's the story of a 31-year-old man who said, "I'm going to start my own business." He did and it ended up bankrupt. So he decided to run for the legislature a year later. He lost. So he started another business. It also went under. Fortunately, though, he met an incredible woman during those trying times. They had fallen in love, and he said, "Forget about politics. Forget about business. I'm going to focus on this beautiful relationship and live on love." During their engagement, she died. He, understandably, had a nervous breakdown and ended up in a rehab clinic at 36. A couple of years later he did what anyone who was institutionalized would do — reentered politics. But this time he ran for Congress. At 43 years of age he lost another election. A few years later, another. And still another. When he was 55, he decided he'd try something new—the Senate. But he lost that election, too. However, his political party thought so much of his tenacity that they nominated him to run as vice president on that year's ticket. But that didn't pan out either. So he decided to run again for the Senate. Unfortunately, he lost again. You never would have heard of him if he had not taken action one more time. At 60 years of age, Abraham Lincoln became the president of the United States.

It's proof that action gets things done. Lincoln never stopped marching forth. He was more than a human *being*. He was a human *doing*. And if you're out doing, you'll never be out done. Lincoln himself wrote, "Always bear in mind that your own resolution to success is more important than any one thing."

MEET FRED

Fred Smith was turned down a hundred times before someone gave him the money to start a delivery company. Someone finally believed in him, and today Federal Express delivers more than a million packages to people everyday. He got there because he absolutely, positively had to be there. The author of *Gone with the Wind* had painful arthritis in her fingers, but her fourth finger obviously was working. Walt Disney went to 302 banks with some Mickey Mouse idea. What if he had stopped at bank number 301? We'd never know Jiminy Cricket, who wrote my favorite axiom: "Accentuate the positive and eliminate the negative."

MEET STEPHEN

Stephen W. Hawkins, regarded as the most brilliant theoretical physicist since Einstein, is also an action taker. Professor Hawkins has a serious degenerative disease which has confined him to a wheelchair for the last 20 years. In 1985 he caught pneumonia and had to have a tracheotomy operation which destroyed his ability to speak. Communicating with the world would be almost impossible for most people in his condition, but the professor instead completed his best-seller landmark book, *A Brief History of Time*. He teaches in a university today, and his life will teach us forever.

MUHAMMAD, MOSES AND MORE

Would we have a prayer if Jesus Christ, Buddha, Muhammad and Moses had not taken action? If Gutenberg had decided action wasn't his type of thing? If Columbus didn't like to travel? It Galileo went to bed before dark? If the Wright Brothers never got off the ground? If Shakespeare wrote only once in a while? If Beethoven hadn't practiced the piano? If Bell was too busy? If Louis Pasteur hadn't taken a shot? No statue was ever erected to the memory of a person who thought it best to leave well enough alone.

There are two kinds of people who don't like taking

action: (1) People who live in the past. They believe that action will cause them to lose something they had before. (2) People who live in the future. They think that taking action will put their future at risk. I might remind both groups that if you keep one foot in the past and one foot in the future, you end up "tinkling" on the present. And the present is where the power is. So march forth by taking action — now.

ACTION AT WORK

The most important action in your work is play. You must play with possibilities. Play with your dreams. And play with your career. It's all a game anyway, isn't it? And if you lose, you just put the pieces back on the board and start again. If you want a raise, tell your boss you want a raise. No one ever got fired for asking for more money. If you want a better job, do a better job and you'll wake up one day running the place.

Now let's say you don't like your job. You're bored. You oversleep a lot so you can be late getting to the office. You're grouchy. You're irritable. You think your boss is a jerk. You think what you're doing is senseless. Now I'm going to tell you what will make you feel better. A raise. You need to raise yourself above your present job and focus on a more exciting one — the job of making yourself happy. Fix up your office with flowers, a smiling picture of yourself. Tack up a sign that says, "Bloom where you're planted." Take on new responsibilities, make new friends and dream a lot.

That's what your job ought to be — a place to work on your dreams. Can you think of a better job than that? Of course, if your work is truly a nightmare, it's time to wake up and take action. In the Bible, there is a section entitled the Book of Job. It is a story of suffering. I sometimes wonder why people pronounce it "Jobe" rather than the more appropriate pronunciation "Job." Yes, there are some people who actually believe they were destined to suffer in their job. Day after day they take no action. To those people, I say, you have no job thinking that way. No job is worth the pay. If you have"dis-ease" in your job, your job will give you a dis-ease. Here, my advice is, if there isn't a good job where you live, move. My wife had a friend who worked day and night at his job at the power company so he could afford to sail every weekend at the lake. She convinced him that if he hooked into his own power to act, he could change his life for the better. He took action and what was once a weekend sail is now a week-long sailing school where he teaches people how to do what he loves — sail and enjoy yourselves.

Years ago while working at an advertising agency in New York, I was told you were really "something" if you had a window office. So I found an office with a window and moved in. I never asked anybody. And no one ever questioned me. Here's my favorite chutzpah story. When movie director Steven Spielberg wanted to break into pictures, he literally broke into a lot at Universal and started directing a picture without permission from the studio. The studio noticed him, recognized his talent and employed him.

There's an old Yiddish proverb that reads, "When man plans, God laughs." I don't think God is laughing because people are making plans. I think God laughs because people make plans but do not take action. When Babbit & Reiman pitches a piece of business, we do a lot more walking than talking. We inundate our prospects with visits, correspondence, phone calls and paraphernalia that let them know how badly we want their business. People may doubt what you say but they believe what you do. So we never, ever stop. We charge more money for our services than any other advertising agency in town. Why? Because we're worth it. How do we get that money? We ask for it. I never understood street people who ask for only a quarter. I have a lot more respect for the ones who have asked me for five and ten dollars. What's more, I give them the money. In business you are very often what you ask for.

Ray Kroc, the founder of McDonald's, was once asked, "If you could give one piece of advice to someone to guarantee long life and success, what would it be?" He said, "Simply remember this: When you're green, you grow; when you're ripe, you rot." What Mr. Kroc meant was that as long as you are curious, as long as you act like a sponge, as long as your soul is a sieve, you will grow and prosper. But if you rest on your laurels, think you know it all, sit back and throw action to the wind, you, too, will end up dust in the wind.

JUST DID IT

One of the most successful advertising campaigns of the 80's was for Nike sneakers. The theme was "Just Do It." This may be the most enlightening message in advertising history. But you don't need the sneakers to make the jump from your job, run circles around the competition or leap into a new field altogether. You win by just doing it. Then you can create your own theme line and put it on a T-shirt — "Just Did It."

Another way of taking action is to downshift. You may want to take this action to reduce the number of things you do in a day. This action is difficult because it bucks the 80's trend, but today success and stress are no longer synonymous. Working long hours is not chic. And conspicuous consumption is out. Bald, bristling men talking to men about manly things over double scotches is passé. The answer to success at work may be doing something that demands less time, less effort, fewer arguments. As Faith Popcorn, founder and chairman of the future-oriented marketing firm Brain-Reserve, concludes, "People will begin to be happy with less. They will become more interested in ethics. They'll go to church or synagogue; they'll get involved with causes; they'll grow their own vegetables. There will be a return to salons — people will get together in groups to talk and enjoy each other's company. They'll be involved in teaching, recycling, and their community. Rather than doing things that cost a lot of money, they'll look to do things that offer gratification to the soul. People will toughen up and become more self-sufficient. We'll turn into a nation of survivors."

The simple life. Yes, it may also mean a smaller paycheck, but the change you get back you will feel forever. So tomorrow, ask the boss how you're doing, but don't forget this — you're the boss. You might want to look back and see how you defined success on page 36. Do you want to reconsider? Make a list before you go any further. List ten things you would like to accomplish in this lifetime.

THINGS TO DO
1.
2.
3.
4.
5.
6.
7.
8.
9.
10.

Make a copy of the proceeding page and keep it next to your bathroom mirror. And be sure to do them all before your time is up.

ACTION IN LOVE

At work, taking action means playing more. But in love, taking action means working more. Love, like everything else, is a choice. And with that choice comes a commitment to work at it every day. Working means giving. Working means nurturing. The business of love never closes.

What would happen if you went to the soil and said, "Give me some fruit." The soil would respond, "Excuse me, but you're a little confused. You must be new. That's not the way it works." The soil explains that first you plant the seed, then you take care of it — water, fertilize, protect and nurture it. And if you do well, you will get the fruit sometime later. You could ask the soil forever, but it wouldn't change its way. You must keep giving and nurturing for the soil to bear fruit. Love grows the same way.

Love begins with loving yourself. Being good to your body, your mind and your soul. Give yourself a hug right now. If that thought seems strange, that's all the more reason to do it. You see, most of us have been denied the person we need the most— ourselves. We desperately need to reestablish this relationship so we know what to do when we have a relationship with someone else.

What we grow up with usually is what we think love is. That love was either nurturing or abusive. As a rule, whoever does not nurture you abuses you. Now keep in mind that no one had a perfect childhood unless their parents were dogs. That's as close to unconditional love as it gets. However, many people have successfully resolved their pasts through self-exploration.

OK, you love yourself. Now you're going to share it with the luckiest person in the world —- the person who loves you. Based on staggering divorce rates in this country, I think it fair to say that most people REACT in their relationships rather than ACT. "He" is taken aback by the horrible things "she" said instead of rubbing her back and helping her find out why she said it. REACTION leads to fights, ultimatums and separations. ACTION leads to trust, intimacy and eternal love.

Most reactions are visitors from the past. Fears disguised as thoughts that make people say, "Well, that's just the way I am," "Love me or leave me," and "You don't understand me." But most of the time you really don't understand you. What's worse is that some of us actually keep mental lists of what's wrong with the other. This is no way to run a relationship. If you start keeping score, the game's over. Action, on the other hand, means sharing your fears, dreams and your life with each other. Action means sharing your souls.

Action means sharing. Doing things together. Remember, love isn't only about looking into each other's eyes. It's about looking in the same direction. My good friends Dr. Arthur and Lois Cohen have bought themselves a swing. They've been married 35 years and still love to dream together, rocking back and forth on their swing. They say there's nothing like it in the world. Cynthia and I purchased one. They are right.

Action means talking. How many times have you been in a restaurant and watched two people sharing a table without a word passing between them? Could the food be so good, or maybe their parents said, "No talking at the dinner table." Here's a tip: If something is on your mind, spill the beans. Keeping it in or keeping your partner out will lead to heartburn and heartbreaks.

Talk about your life, your love, your children, your parents, your in-laws, but just talk. Cynthia and I both have hectic schedules. Still we meet at the same time and the same place every evening to share news about our jobs and to ask each other how we're doing with our relationship. Give yourself a check-up. Check on your lover. Check on your kids. Check on your parents. Check up. Check in, but don't check out.

Action in love also means demonstrating your love. Cynthia is a dedicated, determined and dependable anchorwoman. She always gets her story, and I knew she'd get this one. In 1990, a story came over the wire that there would be a drug bust in the penthouse of Atlanta's tallest building. Cynthia and her news team showed up at the scene of the crime. Surrounding the building were squads of police cars with lights flashing and a Red Dog SWAT team with machine guns loaded. At first they wouldn't let Cynthia into the building but, like always, she persuaded them. Still they informed her that she was risking her life. Cynthia and a bullet-proofed SWAT force took the elevator to the 50th floor, raced down the corridor and broke through the door. But instead of finding Noriega, she found me at a candlelit table for two with a bottle of champagne and an engagement ring. She came thinking that she would get the "story of a lifetime." What she didn't know was that it would be her own.

HEALTH IN ACTION

Action leads to health. Inaction leads to hell. It's that simple. When you take action, you take destiny into your own hands. But many people I have spoken with have trouble marching forth when it comes to their health. I believe this has happened because most of our society is addicted.

People still smoke. My agency had a wonderful idea some years ago. We wanted to find a billboard in a cemetery and write the words "Smoking Section" on it. If you know of one, please send me the address. I'm dying to do it. But not dying as quickly as so many are from cigarette-related diseases. I smoked cigarettes for twenty years. Then I took action. I put them out.

My father died of cancer on a December 4th, so I thought as a gift to him I would quit on that day. I did.

And believe me, cold turkey is not for chickens. It was hard, but the gift I gave to him turned out to be the gift he gave to me. I haven't picked up a cigarette since and never will. Pick a day. Your birthday. Your anniversary. How about March 4th? Smoke your brains out the day before, then look at the cigarette package, put it in the palms of your hands and crush it. Save it to show people that you stopped cancer with your bare hands.

Alcohol is making the world see double. Teenage alcoholism has doubled in the last decade. Drunk driving fatalities have reached double-digit percentages across the country. And it's doubly hard to take action against it. If you think you drink too much, you probably do. If you don't have the courage to seek help, pick up a book on the "12 Steps." In fact, even if you've never had a drink before, you ought to read about the program anyway. I've been told that regardless of your addiction, the "12 Steps" will have you dancing back into life instead of falling into the drink.

The most important step you can take in curing yourself, though, is acknowledging the problem. Taking this action insures success, because you acknowledge an addiction. You're facing it head on. This will allow you to control it instead of it controlling you. Remember, acknowledgment is action.

Overweight people ought to throw out their diets. They're masochistic. Just look what the first three letters of *diet* spell. What overweight people really need is more sugar, as in sweetness in their lives. The emptiness most obese people feed with food can be fed with activities, hobbies, movies, art classes and yoga. Most doctors agree that fat is bad and that we should cut it out. So replace it with sugar. Hug yourself. Kiss the mirror. Tell yourself you're loved. You want to lose weight without losing your mind? Then stop thinking about losing and start thinking about gaining. New friends. New interests. A new goal. What you're looking for is not in the refrigerator.

Exercise is action and it works. Dr. Mark Connolly, cardio-thoracic surgeon at Emory University says, "Regular exercise at least three times a week allows you to enjoy life's three luxuries. Eating, drinking and lovemaking." And you don't need to jump up and down to achieve success. Dancing burns calories and puts you in the mood to take over the world. I try to dance at least once a day. Try it in your underwear at home with the music loud. Also, the latest findings tell us that taking a leisurely walk is just as beneficial as jogging. All good health is based on a state of well-being, so it's important to get motivated.

Now get ready, because this is one of the most important parts of the Hand Book. Most people search all their lives for someone or something to get them motivated. A new hairdo. A new job. A new person. A new-age jazz class. A new way to live our lives. The irony is that you will never be motivated unless you take action first. Underline this: First you take action, then you'll get motivated. Not the other way around.

GOD IN ACTION

Perhaps the greatest action we can take is to move toward faith. It doesn't matter what religion you are. It doesn't even matter if you have a religion. What matters is believing. Faith is the only thing in the world that never changes. If someone says to you, "God isn't near," ask them, "Who moved?" Children often ask if there is a God, why can't they see God. Rabbi Sue Ann Wasserman tells them, "You can't see the wind, electricity or love, but you feel them, don't you? God works the same way. Often through the actions of others."

When my hand was paralyzed after the car accident, a priest came into my hospital room and told me that he had just given Mass and, though I was Jewish, he had prayed for me. He gave me his shoes so I could walk on the road of recovery. He told me that on my walk I would meet Saint Jude, the saint of the impossible and hopeless causes. I took his shoes and, in my heart, I took the walk. I will never forget the feeling of faith I had as I fell asleep that night. Nor will I forget the feeling I had in my fingers the next morning. Though full recovery was more than a year away, I had experienced a miracle. Faith. It is greater than Judaism. Greater than Christianity. It is greater than any religion our world has to offer because it is not of this world.

An interesting sidebar to this story is that I met a Jewish boy from Virginia in that Italian hospital who had suffered a ruptured appendix. Unlike me, who was fortunate to have my mother by my side, neither of his parents was there. This 16-year-old was scared, so my mother and I took care of him. We gave him some much needed faith. When he was ready to leave, not knowing I, too, was Jewish, he told me, "I never knew Christians were so loving." I said, "Thank you."

When you give someone a hand, you are as close to being Godlike as you will be in this lifetime, because that's God's action—giving us a hand. So give of yourself as often as you wish to feel divine. Danny Thomas spent a lifetime raising money and hope for the kids at St. Jude Children's Research Center. His daughter, Marlo, who now continues his mission, says that her father believed there are two kinds of people in this world—the takers and the givers. He said, "The taker's may eat a little better, but the giver's sleep a little better." Whether you use your hand to create a little garden, write a check to your favorite charity, or wipe the tears from another, no action is more sacred or bigger. It's the little things we do that mean so much.

THE LITTLE FINGER MEANS A LOT

Little things take so little energy for all the good they produce. Only when we recognize the little things can we understand the bigger picture, and only when we do little things for others can we appreciate how truly big we are.

Your little finger serves as a little reminder that the little things in life can make a big difference. Emerson said, "The creation of a thousand forests is in one acorn."

There's a story about a time traveler from Wyoming who lived in the year 2020. One day he traveled back millions of years to get a glimpse of the dinosaurs. Time-travel rules stated he could move around all he wanted, but could not step off the ramp of the spaceship. He saw plenty of prehistoric life, including the *Tyrannosaurus rex*. But in his excitement he stepped off the ramp and squashed an ant. An ant who was supposed to mate with another ant. The creatures would have started an ant colony and carried acorns to their ant hill for fortification. Acorns that would have grown into trees. Trees that would have made a forest. A forest that a rich man would own. A man who would have a daughter who would become an environmentalist. An environmentalist who would save the rain forest. But when the time traveler returned to the 21st century, there were no trees anywhere. Just green, steel buildings. Because when the ant was crushed, so was the future of the world.

When I moved to Atlanta, I began a search for the perfect house to buy. My quest would take five years. I found it when I was looking at another house. It was a grand Tudor full of great detail and neat moldings. Yuppies fall for this stuff all the time. The owner almost had me sold, but I couldn't get past the fact that this beautiful house sat on less than a quarter acre of land. In her last-ditch effort to sell me, she said, "Joey, you need the grandest house on the block, not some little cottage like the one down the street." Bingo. I bought that little cottage. All because of that little comment. A cottage, I might add, that sits on two beautiful acres of land filled with wonderful trees. Probably the result of a single acorn.

Nothing is insignificant. Nothing. Little things are the causes of great things. You can take all the darkness in the world, light one candle, and the darkness is gone. It might not be an interview for a job or a romantic date that changes your life. But someone you meet on the way to that interview or to that restaurant may ultimately change your life. Grandpa Fred passed away years ago. He was too young to die, which made me too young to remember him. Grandma Mae, who celebrates her 88th birthday this year, was devastated. She didn't want to meet anyone else for the longest time. My mother was understandably concerned. One spring my mother suggested that she visit my great-grandparents in Phoenix, Arizona. Grandma Mae said it was a bad time to go because Gene, her son, wasn't feeling well. What's more, it would be impossible to get a reservation so quickly. Excuses. Excuses. Excuses.

My mother called the airline. All passages were booked, but there was one seat left on the train which was leaving in two hours. Mom packed Grandma Mae's bags and drove her to the station. My grandmother thought it was the craziest thing she had ever done. The first night on the train the coachman sat my grandmother across from a man named Harry Edison. What started as one extra ticket for a seat on a train turned out to be her ticket to happiness. Harry and Mae would take their next trip together, down the aisle.

Babbit & Reiman has courted many clients and won their business. One of the few pitches we lost — BellSouth Mobility — was lost because the client was mortified by our creative presentation. They saw it as a body of work that broke every rule. I saw it as a breakthrough. BellSouth had these parting words: "Who do you think we are? PacTel Cellular?" They were the competition and my next phone call. I called PacTel's president, presented the work and before the trade papers could print our loss of BellSouth Mobility, we had announced the win of PacTel Cellular. Just a little comment that changed the world for me that day.

The point of these little stories is simple — grab the moment and cherish all it has to offer. Each moment is like a cell in our body—it may be small but it contains all the information in the world. Sherlock Holmes built his entire career on looking out for little things, so we ought not forget his tenet—it's elementary.

One good word can rewrite someone's life into a hit. In college, I wrote a paper for an American studies course entitled "Class Struggle in America." My peers wrote treatises on the subject. Well-researched, well-documented papers. I, on the other hand, read Phillip

Roth's *Portnoy's Complaint* and one book by Stephen Birmingham and deduced the following hypothesis: If you're wealthy and born Christian, you eventually become Jewish. But if you're wealthy and born Jewish, you eventually become Christian. The title of my paper was "Don't Tell Anyone, But Jackie O. Is Really Jewish." The paper received a B+ with the following critique from the professor: "Mr. Reiman, your qualitative and quantitative data is irrelevant. Your conclusion is far fetched, if not preposterous. But boy, can you write!" Those last five words changed my life. I had been given the thumbs-up. With a stroke of a pen, I had become a writer.

People always ask me how to get into advertising. What courses should they take in college? What college should they attend? Who should they talk to? What should they do? (Lots of *shoulds* — be careful.) Well, here's how I did it. I was waiting for a bus. I missed the first one when a woman started talking to me about job interviewing. She said a certain place needed typists. I figured if they needed typists they must need writers for the typists. She told me it was an advertising agency. I've been making headlines ever since. So next time you miss a bus, that doesn't mean you've missed out.

Now, little things can also cause a little misery. I always tell people who are interviewing for a job that if they have the wrong name, things can't go right. Here's what I mean. If your name is Bob and you interview with a woman who just divorced her husband whose name is Bob, what do you think her first impression of you will be when you say, "My name is Bob. Glad to meet you"? Or worse yet, the person interviewing you might have hemorrhoids. Then you're in real trouble.

Little things get even a little stickier when you hear something bad about a person. People say, "Where there's smoke, there's a fire." Richard Nixon, Gary Hart, and Jim and Tammy Bakker have all gotten into big trouble because of little things they missed or a little thing someone said.

On a happier note, let me share the story of how this book came about. One day I ordered new checks from the bank. The checks never came to my house. They were delivered instead to the home of Robyn Spizman, one of Atlanta's top talk-show personalities, author and book promoter. When she saw the blank checks with my name on them, she suddenly remembered a speech I had given and thought, "He's got to write a book based on that speech." Robyn came to my office and told me of her plan. I looked at the checks and reveled in the idea that we all write our own check for the amount of good fortune we want in our lives. Looking back, that episode wasn't a postal mix up. It was a special delivery. Or as Dante put it, "From a little spark bursts a mighty flame."

Little things are divided into two groups. The first group includes the little things we hear, see or do that change our lives. The second group is the little things we do for ourselves or someone we care about. Have you ever had your day turn around because of one cheerful word? Just try it. One little word of encouragement is worth more than all the words in the dictionary. A smile to another person is like sunshine to a flower. And the glow of a warm thought is more comforting than money. Yes, little things do add up, and though for the moment they might add just a little happiness or misery, their sum has a major consequence. As small as it may be, think of your pinkie as the finger that can actually put someone in the pink. Remember these little things:

The Smile

The most powerful tool known to civilization is the smile. It takes a whole bunch of muscles to make one, but it takes only one happy thought. I am convinced that the smile muscles are connected to nerves which connect to a warehouse of happy, healthy chemicals kept in the brain, and when you smile these chemicals spill throughout your body. A frown, on the other hand, ought to be outlawed along with handguns. It kills every time. Next time someone frowns at you, smile back. It's the best weapon against a frown. And if you give a smile, you might get one back.

The Phone Call

Call the ones you care about and tell them you were

thinking of them. AT&T made a fortune by telling people to reach out and touch someone. The reason the campaign did so well is because it's true. When you call someone, you do touch someone. Imagine that, truth in advertising. I call my wife five times a day to tell her I love her. She does the same. This way no matter where we are or where we travel, it never seems like long distance. It's the same way in business. If you call your clients every day, they'll never have any hangups with you. One more kind of call is crucial — the one to yourself. You'll need an answering machine, though. Call yourself and leave a message like this: "Welcome home. Take a deep breath. That's it. Now let it out. Let go of everything. Just savor how wonderful it is to feel alive. All fears are gone. All the wonders are yours. You are recharged and renewed." Leave a positive message on your machine every day. When you get home you'll hear the answer to the problem you might have thought up during the day.

The Postcard

OK, you don't like to write letters. But what about postcards? If you have something nice to say, a postcard not only lets that person know you care but also sends the same message to all the nosy people who read it. Cynthia and I keep lots of postcards around and send them *post haste* after a nice thought about someone in particular hits us.

The Thank-You Note

Absolutely mandatory. We have a friend named Janet Gaffney. No matter what occasion of ours she comes to, we receive a thank-you note within 48 hours. She even sends us a note when we go to her house. In fact, any interaction with Janet produces a thank-you note in our mailbox. I'm convinced Janet's heart is full of thoughts for others. As a result, she is in our hearts and in this book.

Happy Birthday

As you know, my advertising agency is closed on March 4th to celebrate marching forth. It is also closed on your birthday. Not Lincoln's. Not Washington's. Christopher Columbus isn't as important as you, either. He may have discovered America 500 years ago, but you're discovering something new every day. He's history. You're the present, and the agency's present to you is to enjoy yourself unencumbered by meetings, schedules and events. Remember, a birthday card is a birthday cake without the mess. It says you count in this world. So be sure to write people's birthdays next to their addresses. Use the last line of the address column. Birthdays are more important than zip codes.

Hugs

There's nothing in the world more wonderful than a hug. How come we don't do it more? It feels so good and it's so easy. But don't wait for people to hug you.

Hug yourself and tell yourself how much you care about yourself. Then hug someone you love and tell them the same. Oh, when you hug someone, make sure you're the last to let go.

Trees

If you're fortunate enough to be around trees, go hug them. Our Native Americans hugged trees all the time. They believed there were good spirits inside them. My close friend Michael Gaffney concurs: "Because we are God's most flawed creation, we have angels to watch over us. Angels aren't abstract beings. Angels live in trees. You can see them if you'll simply go and look."

Watercolors

I'm convinced that heaven is painted in watercolors, because it feels like heaven to paint with them. I am not a painter, but I love the look, the feel and life of watercolor art. No oils or charcoal or expensive canvas is needed. All you need is a basic set of paints, some paper and a beautiful patch of nature. Then just add water. They make great presents and it's terrific therapy for yourself.

Flowers

Grow them. Emerson said, "The earth laughs in flowers." Send them often, even if you don't have a reason. They look, feel and smell beautiful. I've been told if you smell roses but there are none in sight, you are in the presence of the Virgin Mary. But don't wait for her. Pick up some flowers now and they'll pick you up. One of my favorite things to do is to send my wife 11 roses with a card that says, "You're number 12."

Camp

When I was 10 I went to a summer camp. The man who ran the place we called Manny. Every Friday night Manny would address the whole camp with a little something. I'll never forget one something he said — "Play it by ear." This little saying will help keep you from getting into big trouble. It means to go with the flow because you can't change anything except how you feel. Change is the only thing that will never change, or as Heraclitus said to his campers in Greece around 6th century B.C., "You can't step twice in the same river."

Cab Drivers

Cab drivers have seen it all, so it should come as no surprise that they know it all. I think they are some of the wisest people in the world. Joel Babbit told me about a little tip he got from a cab driver. I never forgot it, and you won't either. It has to do with people who think they have fame, fortune and power — people like Leona Helmsley, John Gotti and Charles Keating, all of whom at this writing are now in jail. As the cabbie so eloquently put it, "No one's cool."

Grandparents

Older people always have little things to say that can make a big difference. My favorite is something my grandfather Opa always said: "There's nothing in life like a good scare." What he was defining was the feeling we get when we think we are sick but we aren't. First you think the world is coming to an end, so you get your values in order. The little things become a lot more important than the ones we think are big. You don't care what you've got in your pocket. All you want is what you can fit in your heart. Life becomes precious and then you find out you're going to be OK. Wouldn't it be nice if we didn't have to scare ourselves into being happy? We don't, you know.

Made vs. Paid

Looking for a gift? Here's some advice. Something made by hand is worth more than a handful of money. Oma, who was married to Opa, used to bake Vanilla Almond Crescents. When I smelled these cookies, I knew I was loved, because she had made them with her own hands for me. Oma was from Vienna, Austria, so her recipe was very special. I had it translated for you:

1 1/4 cups flour	2 egg yolks
3/4 cup butter	1/3 cup sugar
1/2 cup blanched & grated almonds	
1/4 cup vanilla sugar	

Work flour, butter, almonds, egg yolks and sugar to a dough. Form small crescents and bake at 300 degrees for 15 – 20 minutes. Dip in vanilla sugar while still hot.

To this day, I cherish things that are made by others, rather than paid for by others.

Teachers

People don't remember their schools or their classes nearly as much as they remember their teachers. Professors Jerry Cohen and Stephen Whitfield of Brandeis University were invaluable to my creative training. Fellini was inspirational, and under the creative directorship of Alvin Hampel, I soared. But it was my sixth-grade teacher, Marvin Terban, who taught me about a little man named Ivan Capp. And it was Ivan Capp who taught me how to write. You see, the letter "I" stands for interjection, "V" for verb, "A" for adjective, "N" for noun, "C" for conjunction, "A" for adverb, "P" for preposition and "P" for pronoun. The lesson is that good teachers never fail you.

A Little Karma

Some people believe in karma, or the energy generated by the actions you take. Even the little ones. It works like a boomerang. Whatever you throw out comes back to you. Throw a punch and you will fall. Throw a kiss and you will be loved. Perhaps karma is the way the universe keeps score. A smile, a thank-you or a compliment gets you one point. Sharing with someone less fortunate gets you five and giving to someone who will never know it was you who gave gets you 100 points. I do believe it all comes back. As the adage goes, "Blessed is he who gives without remembering, takes without forgetting."

Little Little Things

The next time you write a check, try this: On the line where it says memo, write the words "Thank You." After all, aren't you thankful for your electricity, your phone, your heat and your home? Even to your bank for lending you money? They deserve to be thanked. What's more, once you thank them they become friends instead of enemies. It's true. When you love something you are its commander, and when you hate something you are its slave. Also, don't forget to buy yourself a gift every week. And always insist that the store giftwrap your present. It's going to the most important person in the world — you — so it must be wrapped beautifully. You'll find that opening your own present gives you the same, if not better, feeling of opening a present from someone else. Toasting is another forgotten art. When dining with anyone, toast to them and to life. Some of my favorite toasts are, "May everything you wish for be the least you get," and "Here's to living every day of our lives." Dining alone? Toast all the people who wish they were dining with you. Oh, never forget this one: Be nice until 10:00 AM and the rest of the day will take care of itself.

The little things in life usually hold the biggest things life has to offer. But they will slip through our fingers if we are not aware. Aware of our good fortune to be alive. Aware of others. Aware of nature. And aware of the moment. The now. If we move so fast that we can't smell the roses, climb the trees or float in the ocean, we will fall out of sync with the world and consequently with ourselves. Helen Keller sees it this way: "I who am blind can give one hint to those who see: use your eyes as if tomorrow you will have been stricken blind. Hear the music of voices, the song of a bird, the mighty strains of an orchestra as if you would be stricken deaf tomorrow. Touch each object as if tomorrow your tactile sense would fail. Smell the perfume of flowers, taste with relish each morsel, as if tomorrow you could never taste or smell again. Make the most of every sense. Glory in all the facets and pleasures and beauty which the world reveals to you."

The journey for personal fulfillment cannot be taken in the fast lane, because in speeding through life, we miss the little things that make up life itself. As my mother always told me, "The journey is always better than the inn."

FINGER TIPS

Thumbs up, pointed forward and fear behind, we march forth knowing that every great journey begins with a little step.

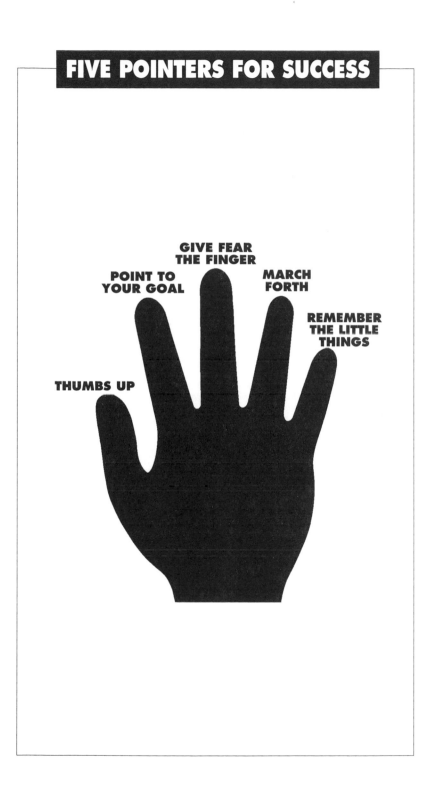

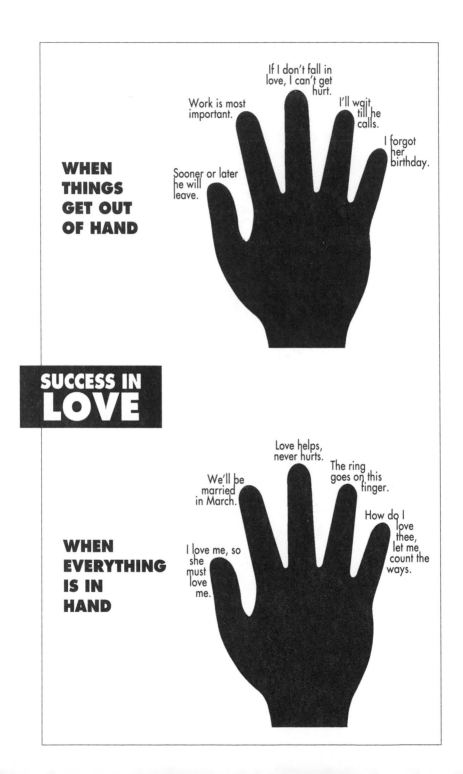

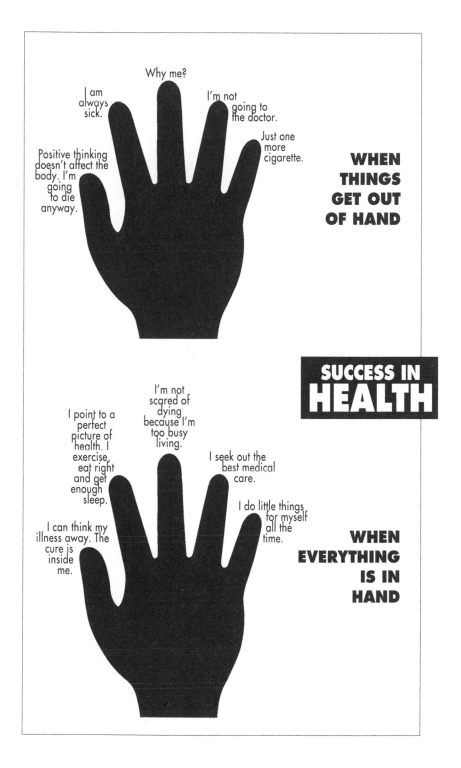

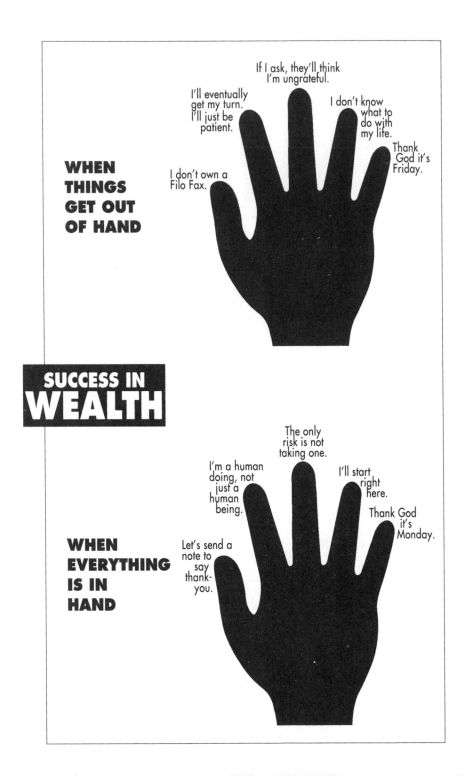

A PRAYER FOR TWO HANDS

If you want something, put your hands together or hold another so there are two hands and say:

I am doubly positive that what I focus on happens because I make fear double over, I take action twice as fast, and I know, now, that I pick the whole world up with my pinkie.

Success is in my hands. I am the creator of my own destiny. I know success is now within my reach.

You're welcome to write to me.

Joey Reiman

Babbit & Reiman Advertising

One Buckhead Plaza

3060 Peachtree Road, NW

Penthouse

Atlanta, GA 30305

I hope this Hand Book will help you hold on to your dreams by living them, point you in the right direction by keeping your heart and mind focused, help you overcome your fears by grasping faith, and encourage you to think bigger by recognizing life's precious little things. Most important, I hope it shows you that if you follow this blueprint, life really works.

Everyone is looking for answers out there. But it is your hand that holds them all. So let it be a constant reminder from this day forth that if you want something, anything, all you have to do is pick it up.

NOW GIVE YOURSELF A BIG HAND!

OTHER BOOKS TO GET YOUR HANDS ON

No book is written without the help of others. These authors gave me a hand and I'm sure they'll give you one, too.

Brown, H. Jackson, Jr. *Life's Little Instruction Book*. Nashville, Tenn.: Rutledge Hill Press, Inc., 1991.

Covey, Stephen R. *The Seven Habits of Highly Effected People*. New York: Simon & Schuster, 1989.

Dass, Ram. *Journey of Awakenings*. New York: Bantam Press, 1990.

De Mello, Anthony. *Awareness*. New York: Doubleday, 1990.

Goleman, Daniel, Paul Kaufman, and Michael Ray. *The Creative Spirit*. New York: Penguin Books, 1992.

Kushner, Harold. *Who Needs God*. New York: Summit Books, 1989.

Lowen, Alexander. *Fear of Life*. New York: Macmillan Publishing Company, 1980.

McWilliams, Peter, and John-Roger. *Life 101*. Los Angeles: Prelude Press, Inc., 1991.

McWilliams, Peter, and John-Roger. *You Can't Afford the Luxury of a Negative Thought*. Los Angeles: Prelude Press, Inc., 1989.

Peck, Scott M. *The Road Less Traveled*. New York: Simon & Schuster, 1978.

Wilde, Stuart. *Affirmations*. Taos, New Mexico: White Dove International, Inc., 1987.

Williams, Margery. *The Velveteen Rabbit*. New York: Doubleday, 1991.

Williamson, Marianne. *Return to Love*. New York: Harper Collins, 1992.

ABOUT THE AUTHOR

Joey Reiman is chairman and chief executive officer of Babbit & Reiman Advertising.

Founded in 1986, the agency has grown at one of the most dramatic rates of any new advertising agency in the United States, with 1992 billings in excess of $80 million and offices in Atlanta and New York. B&R has won more than 300 creative awards in national and international competitions and has been featured in *The Wall Street Journal*, *The New York Times*, and *USA Today*.

A graduate of Brandeis University, Joey was previously executive vice president of D'Arcy McManus & Masius, Atlanta, and prior to that he worked in New York at Grey Advertising and Benton Bowles. His clients have included Cadillac, CBS News, Coca-Cola, Colgate/Palmolive, Days Inn, GTE, General Tire, Lanier Business Systems, M&M Mars, Procter & Gamble, Turner Broadcasting, and USA Today.

Joey is also one of this country's most popular motivational speakers. He has been invited to America's largest and most prestigious conventions and organizations to share his philosophy and stories. He authored the musical *Discovery — The True Story of Christopher Columbus*, studied filmmaking in Italy under director Federico Fellini, and has recently written *The Princess Problem*, a full-length ballet. In 1987, Joey founded ORFUN, a non-profit organization that raises money for emotionally battered children. Joey also sits on the board of directors of the Alliance Theatre, the American Red Cross, the Cystic Fibrosis Foundation, and St. Jude Children's Research Hospital.

Joey and his wife, Cynthia, live in Atlanta with their horse, Holly, and their cat, Henry.